Seasonal Quilts
Using Quick Bias

GRETCHEN K. HUDOCK

Martingale®
& COMPANY

Credits

CEO · *Daniel J. Martin*

President · *Nancy J. Martin*

Publisher · *Jane Hamada*

Editorial Director · *Mary V. Green*

Managing Editor · *Tina Cook*

Technical Editor · *Ellen Pahl*

Copy Editor · *Durby Peterson*

Design Director · *Stan Green*

Illustrator · *Laurel Strand*

Cover and Text Designer · *Trina Stahl*

Photographer · *Brent Kane*

That Patchwork Place® is an imprint of
Martingale & Company®.

Seasonal Quilts Using Quick Bias
© 2004 by Gretchen K. Hudock

Martingale & Company
20205 144th Avenue NE
Woodinville, WA 98072-8478 USA
www.martingale-pub.com

Printed in China
09 08 07 06 05 04   8 7 6 5 4 3 2 1

Mission Statement

Dedicated to providing quality products and service to inspire creativity.

Library of Congress Cataloging-in-Publication Data

Hudock, Gretchen K.
    Seasonal quilts using quick bias / Gretchen K. Hudock.
        p. cm.
    "That Patchwork Place."
    ISBN 1-56477-545-3
    1. Appliqué—Patterns, 2. Quilting—Patterns
3. Seasons in art. 4. Fusible materials in sewing.
I. Title.
    TT779.H84 2004
    746.46'o41—dc

2004003599

Dedication

To my family: Rich, John, and Elizabeth

Acknowledgments

Many people have helped make this book a reality. I'd like to express my thanks to:
Kate Bashynski, Betty Hanneman, and Susan Petruske for taking my concepts and
turning them into wonderful projects.

Laure Noe for creating workable illustrations from my hand-drawn sketches.

Mary Kotek for her editing expertise and hand quilting.

Jan Carr and Clover Needlecraft Inc. for creating a product
that continues to give me inspiration.

Martingale & Company for making it possible for me to share my designs and ideas.

My coworkers for their support, encouragement, and constructive advice.

And special thanks to my husband, Rich, for his patience, love, and understanding while
I worked on the book. It is safe to come into the sewing room now!

Contents

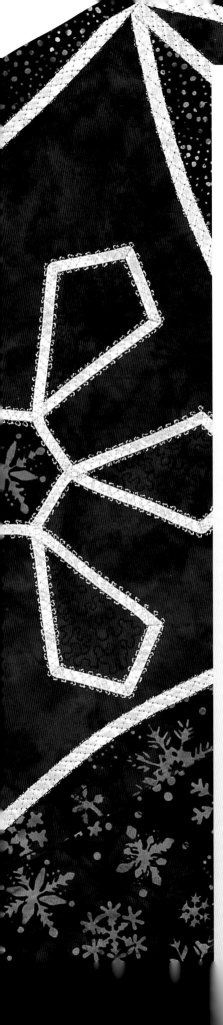

Introduction

QUILTERS LOVE PRODUCTS that simplify tasks when making quilts. Quick Bias, a fusible-bias tape manufactured by Clover, is one such product. This ready-made bias tape eliminates the time-consuming cutting and piecing needed to create long bias strips for appliqué. We can now simply press and stitch, focusing on fun and creativity. Curved designs are no longer a scary thought; they are welcomed for adding just the perfect accent to many projects.

The Quick Bias family of tapes is easy to use, and all the basic techniques needed to complete the projects in this book are found in "Quick Bias Basics" beginning on page 7. One of the wonderful attributes of Quick Bias projects is that their size can be changed with ease. With the help of a copy machine, most of the designs can be customized to fit any size needed. The Mini Bias can be used in a small design, and when the design is enlarged, the standard size Quick Bias will then work.

Most of us who quilt enjoy making items to decorate our homes for the seasons. Following "Quick Bias Basics," I've included a section called "Designing Your Own Seasonal Quilts." Read through it and learn how to vary the designs in this book to create your own unique projects. I've also included a discussion on borders, providing ideas and inspiration for customizing the projects. Finally, the projects illustrate how to put all the various components together to create easy, one-of-a-kind items for your home or for gifts. Your project will be as unique as a snowflake! (I've even included three snowflake designs!) You can make everything from a small ornament to a large tree skirt and anything in between.

Many quilt shops now carry the Quick Bias family of tapes, but if you have trouble finding it, check "Resources" on page 96 for mail-order information. There are many colors available in the ready-made tapes. If you find you really love working with fusible bias, you can purchase a Fusible Bias Tape Maker and create your own bias tape in widths ranging from ¼" to 1".

The techniques and designs in this book are focused on quilts and quilted projects, but feel free to use the Quick Bias, Mini Bias, and Border Bias to simplify and embellish other sewing projects as well. Wearable art and home decorating projects can also be enhanced using the bias tapes. Use the various tapes to have some fun and map your own route in quilting. I hope you will become as "biased" for Quick Bias as I am!

Quick Bias Basics

THE BASICS ARE always important when learning new techniques. Take some time to read the following guidelines—they will save you time later. Ready, set, go!

Gathering Your Supplies

All of the supplies needed to make the projects in this book are readily available at your local fabric store or quilt shop; if not, see "Resources" on page 96.

The bias family. The ready-made bias tapes come in spools of 5½ yards and 11 yards. Each project in this book lists an approximate amount needed. Bias tapes come in three different widths and a wide range of colors; they are 100% cotton (except for the metallic tapes, which are 100% polyester). A strip of fusible web is centered on the back of the tape, but does not extend to the edges. This makes it possible to stitch the tape down along the edges without gumming up the needle. Once stitched in place, the bias tapes are washable and dry-cleanable.

Fabric. The best fabric choice for Quick Bias projects is 100% cotton. Cotton blends and other fibers may not withstand the heat needed to apply the bias correctly. Because of the seasonal nature of the projects, you can take advantage of the many fun novelty prints readily available for each season. The prints should be small to medium in scale, depending on the size of the finished item. Textured solids, batiks, and marbled fabrics also work very well. For a no-sew alternative to cottons for the appliqués, you can also use synthetic suede.

Yardage requirements for all the projects are based on 40" of usable fabric, after washing and preshrinking. Apply a spray sizing to the wrong

Quick Bias Tape Spools

side of the fabrics to replace body lost during washing, and press all fabrics before you begin.

Paper. Use plain white copy paper or semitransparent paper for tracing the designs from the book.

Nonpermanent pencil or fabric marker, or carbonless transfer paper and transfer wheel. The tool to use for transferring the design to the fabric depends on the transfer method you choose (see "Transferring the Design" on page 11). The marking tools I prefer include a fine-tip, water-soluble marker for light-colored fabrics and a soapstone marker or fine-tip, chalk-type marker for dark-colored fabrics. Marks made with these products remove easily if you need to correct a mistake.

Sew-through paper-backed fusible web or temporary spray adhesive. You will need one of these products to apply appliqué shapes or other fabric to the background material.

Batting. Choose low-loft cotton, cotton-polyester, or polyester battings for these projects. I prefer dense, low-loft, needle-punched polyester batting because it provides stability, especially for wall quilts. Avoid high-loft battings. Since the bias is applied after layering, the loftier batting makes it more difficult to apply and stitch down the bias tape.

Sewing machine needles. A size 80/12 universal needle is suitable for almost all of the required stitching. The stitching performs two functions at the same time: quilting and attaching the bias tape, so a smaller needle is not recommended. Double needles can be used to stitch down both edges of the tape when stitching on straight areas or on very gentle curves. A 4.0/90 double needle is used for the Quick Bias and a 3.0/90 for the Mini Bias. A size 80/12 metallic or machine-embroidery needle can be used when working with specialty threads, if necessary, to achieve a balanced stitch.

Thread. Any color thread can be used to stitch down the bias strips. Sometimes I want the stitching to blend in with the bias tape, so I use a color that matches. Other times I use a contrasting thread, as the stitching on the bias tape is part of the design of the project. In most cases, a 50-weight cotton works well. Rayon, metallic, or monofilament thread may also be used for stitching down the bias tapes. Use a 50-weight thread for all piecing.

Mini-iron or iron. A conventional iron is fine, but the mini-iron's small heated surface is ideal for fusing the bias pieces into place, and it is easier to manipulate than a conventional iron.

Stiletto. Use this tool to help manipulate the bias tape around corners and angles.

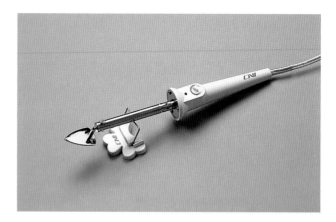

Mini-Iron

Portable pressing surface. A small pressing surface is very handy. It makes fusing the bias tape easy because you can simply turn the pressing surface rather than reposition the project while applying the bias tape.

Rotary-cutting equipment. Use a rotary cutter, ruler, and mat for normal cutting tasks. The rotary ruler is also helpful when applying bias tape in straight lines to make sure the tape is straight and parallel to any seams or other bias tape.

Fusible-Bias Options

There are three widths of fusible-bias tapes to choose from: Mini Bias, Quick Bias, and Border Bias. Which to select? It's nice to have choices, and a little background information may help you determine what is best for your project. Basically the smaller the project, the narrower the bias tape, but there are always exceptions! You want the bias tape to be proportionate to the finished item. Sometimes you may want to use two parallel rows of Mini Bias with spacing in between, or use just one row of Quick Bias. On large projects, you may wish to use the Border Bias or two rows of Quick Bias. When it comes to colors, you can choose the appropriate color or use the variegated bias and cut different sections from the color palette to get a variety of colors.

Mini Bias, Quick Bias, and Border Bias

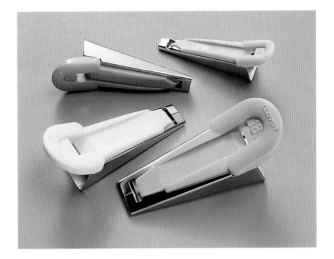

Fusible Bias Tape Makers

Mini Bias is approximately ⅛" wide. It is wonderful for smaller designs and more intricate curves. It comes in a variety of colors and in metallic. In this book, use the Mini Bias for projects using blocks smaller than 8" square, such as the ornaments or door pillows, or as border designs on some pillows.

Quick Bias is ¼" wide. It works well for a variety of sizes, but 8" blocks or larger are the best choice.

Border Bias is ¾" wide. It can be used on large quilts as vines in borders or as a binding treatment on curved edges. I also use it on smaller projects with a contrasting decorative stitch or with Mini Bias stitched down the center of the bias tape to make it look like narrower bias.

Making Your Own Fusible-Bias Tape

There are times when you need a bias-tape color that is not available in ready-made tape. This is when you may want to create your own fusible bias with the Fusible Bias Tape Maker. This tool is similar to the traditional bias-tape maker, but it has an attachment on the top through which the fusible tape is fed. As you pull and press both the fabric and the tape through the tool, the tape becomes fused to the fabric. Very cool!

There are five sizes of tape makers available: ¼", ⅜", ½", ¾", and 1". There are two sizes of fusible tape to use with them. The smaller tape fits the ¼" and ⅜" tape makers, and the larger fits the three larger sizes: ½", ¾", and 1".

QUICK TIP

If you are using the finished fusible tape to cover straight design lines, it is not necessary to cut the fabric strip on the bias. Use simple straight-grain strips in the correct width and proceed with the directions. You must cut strips on the bias for any curved lines.

---

1. Cut your fabric strips on the bias in the width required. You may need to piece occasionally to get the needed length, but do not feel that you must have one complete piece to finish your project. There are often times when you can tuck the raw edge of one piece under an intersecting piece of bias and use smaller pieces. If piecing is necessary, place the strips perpendicular to each other, right sides

together, and offset them as shown. Sew together using a ¼" seam allowance. Press the seam open and trim to a scant ⅛". Press again.

2. Hold the Fusible Bias Tape Maker with the attachment side face up. Insert the end of the fusible tape through the attachment, paper side up. Thread the tape through the guide and out the front. Leave about ½" extending beyond the opening.

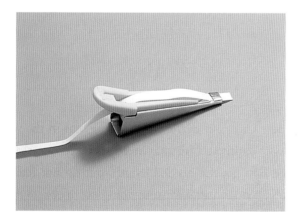

3. Cut an angled edge on the bias fabric strip to make it easier to feed. Turn the bias-tape maker over and insert the strip through the metal opening, right side up. Use a stiletto or awl to help feed the fabric through the

opening. When the fabric is visible near the front opening, use your fingers to pull it out about 1".

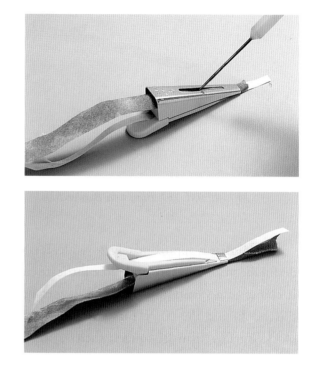

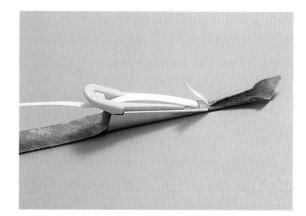

4. Turn the bias-tape maker over once again and lift the fusible tape up so that you can see the folded fabric underneath. Make sure that the raw edges of the fabric strip are centered as it comes through the opening. It can be tweaked a bit to center it prior to pressing.

5. Once the strip is centered and the fusible tape is in place, place the tape maker flat on your ironing surface with the metal side down. I am right-handed so I place the tape maker on the far right side of my ironing surface. Secure the

ends of the fusible web and the fabric by inserting two single pins or a fork pin through both the fabric and fusible web into the ironing surface.

6. When the ends are secure, hold the tab on the end of the tape maker and begin pulling gently while pressing the fusible web and fabric coming out of the other side. Always keep a firm hold on the tab to maintain tension on the fusible bias as it cools. Keep checking the fabric strip before it feeds through the tape maker to see that it is lying flat for feeding.

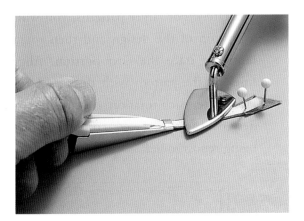

7. Once you have enough tape made, or when you no longer have room to press any more fusible bias, put the mini-iron on its stand or set your iron aside. Continue to hold the tab to maintain tension on the strip until it cools. The fusible agent liquefies as you iron, and it needs to cool down and solidify before you let go of the tab. If you do not do this, the tape will bubble up, and your strip will not perform well. This cooling takes just 20 to 30 seconds. I usually rub my right hand lightly over the tape while I hold the tab, so I can tell if it is cool. Once the fusible tape has cooled, unpin the secure end and remove it from the tape

maker by pulling out any remaining tape and fabric from the front.

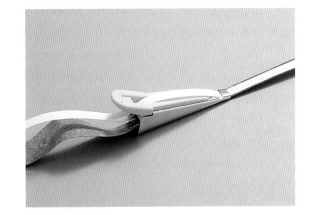

8. When you are ready to use the bias tape, remove the paper side of the web and proceed as directed in "Applying the Bias Tape" on page 18.

Transferring the Design

Transferring the design to the background fabric is the first step in making any of the projects in this book. This transferred design will help you position appliqués and bias tape. Use a copy machine to reduce or enlarge the designs as needed. The designs can be made into many different sizes, depending on what type of project you are making. Some patterns are printed as a quarter of the design because the full size is too large for the book page. The directions for specific projects in the book will tell you how much to reduce or enlarge a pattern. In addition, I've included tables on pages 30–31 with percentages for reducing and enlarging the designs to fit specific sizes of blocks.

Choose from two methods of transferring the design to the background fabric. In Method I, you place the pattern under the fabric and trace using a light box and nonpermanent marker. In Method II, you place the pattern over the fabric and use carbonless transfer paper.

Method I
Fabric on Top

1. Photocopy the pattern for the seasonal design and border, if applicable, from the book or trace the pattern onto a piece of paper. Be sure to include all lines and seam allowances if required. Solid lines indicate placement for fabric pieces and bias strips; dashed lines are for alignment purposes. Small stars indicate the center point of the design and borders for placement.

2. Tape the photocopied or traced pattern to a light box or window. You can also use a table that pulls apart for extension leaves by placing a sheet of glass over the opening and putting a lamp (with the shade removed) underneath.

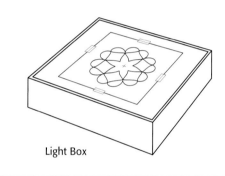

Light Box

QUICK TIP

If you have a plastic extension table for your sewing machine, you can use it for a light box. Place a light under it and tape the pattern to the table.

3. Fold the background fabric in half twice to mark the quarters of your fabric. Gently press the folds. The creases will help you align the pattern and fabric. If you want the design to be square, fold lengthwise and widthwise. If you want the design on point, fold diagonally from corner to corner.

4. With right side up, place the fabric over the pattern, aligning the creases on the fabric with the corresponding lines on the pattern, if necessary. Tape down the edges of the fabric just enough to keep it from shifting while tracing but not enough to make it difficult to remove if you need to reposition the fabric.

5. Using a nonpermanent pencil or fabric marker, trace the design onto the fabric. Use a clear acrylic ruler to trace straight lines accurately. For larger patterns, you will trace a portion of the design and then rotate the fabric to trace the next portion. Align the lines on the pattern with the creases on the fabric after each rotation. Most of the smaller designs can be traced completely without being repositioned.

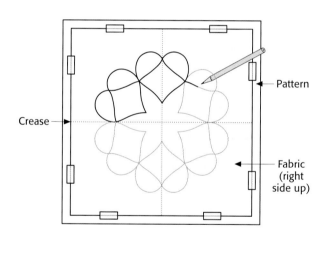

Pattern

Crease

Fabric (right side up)

QUICK TIP

If it is difficult to see the design through dark fabrics, retrace the pattern with a bold line to make it more visible.

Method II
Pattern on Top

For this method, you will need carbonless transfer paper and a tracing wheel.

1. Follow steps 1 and 3 of Method I.

2. Lay the background fabric, right side up, on a flat surface. Tape it in place around the edges, using just enough tape so the fabric doesn't shift.

3. Place a sheet of carbonless transfer paper, transfer side down, over the fabric.

4. Place the traced pattern over the fabric and transfer paper, aligning the creases of the fabric with the corresponding lines on the pattern. Tape the pattern in place, using just enough tape to keep the pattern from shifting while tracing, but not enough to make it difficult to remove when you need to reposition the pattern.

5. Using a tracing wheel, trace over the design to transfer it to the fabric. Once you have traced the portion of the design contained on the pattern, rotate the pattern and transfer paper to trace the next portion as needed to complete the design. Align the lines on the pattern with the creases on the fabric after each rotation. Refer to the project instructions and the diagram given with each design for additional guidance.

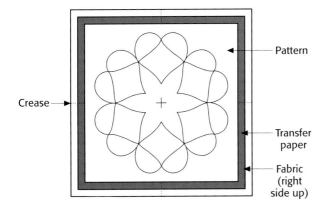

Crease

Pattern

Transfer paper

Fabric (right side up)

Adding Appliqués

Once a design is chosen, the next step is to add any fabric pieces and appliqué shapes to the background. In this book, most of the fabric pieces added to the background will be used as either an appliqué design or in the border area.

Fabrics are applied to the background temporarily and then stitched down permanently when the bias tape is fused and stitched. To temporarily hold your fabric appliqué pieces in place, you can use either paper-backed fusible web or temporary spray adhesive. Adhesive spray gives a softer appearance to the finished quilt, but fusible web is more secure when stitching. With fusible web there is less likelihood of the pieces shifting while they are being stitched down. Use fusible web in a sew-through weight for cotton fabrics and a heavier, no-sew weight if you are using synthetic suede for the appliqué.

Fusible-Web Method

1. Trace the required number of each shape onto the paper side of the fusible web, leaving a small amount of space between the pieces. There is no need to make a mirror image of any of the pieces used for the designs in this book. Be as accurate as possible when tracing.

QUICK TIP

To save time, trace like pieces together and oriented in the same direction so they can all be placed on the straight of grain when they are fused to the fabric.

---

2. Roughly cut around each individual shape or, if there are several of the same shape and fabric, cut around each group.

Fusible web (paper side up)

3. Follow the manufacturer's instructions to fuse the traced shapes onto the wrong side of the appropriate fabric. Try to position the shapes so they will be cut on the straight grain whenever possible. Let cool after fusing. Cut out each individual shape along the drawn lines and remove the paper backing.

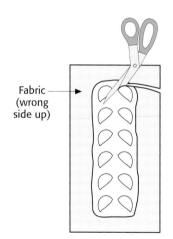

Fabric (wrong side up)

4. Arrange the pieces on the background fabric, following the pattern or project instructions. Once you are pleased with the placement, follow the manufacturer's instructions to fuse the pieces in place.

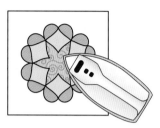

QUICK TIP

Trace any interior design lines—such as on the egg, pumpkin, leaf, or basket—onto the paper side of the fusible web with a dark pen. Once the web is fused to the chosen fabric and roughly cut out, transfer the interior lines to the front of the fabric by placing the shape on a light box and tracing them lightly onto the right side of the fabric. Apply Mini Bias or machine satin stitch these lines to highlight and accent the designs.

TEMPORARY-SPRAY-ADHESIVE METHOD

1. Make a paper template for each of the patterns needed by tracing the design onto paper. Make one of each pattern, as the template can be used multiple times. The type of paper does not matter, but I like to use an iron-on grid

paper called Grid Grip. It helps me align the templates on the straight of grain and eliminates pinning the template to the fabric while cutting.

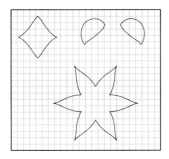

2. From the appropriate fabric(s), cut a piece of fabric slightly larger than the template. Cut the desired number of fabric pieces and stack them together, right sides up. Pin or iron the template to the top piece. Be careful not to overly press if you are using iron-on paper templates. Cut out the shapes from the fabrics, cutting as many pieces at one time as you can. Reuse the template as necessary.

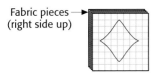

Fabric pieces (right side up)

3. Place one of the fabric shapes on a piece of scrap paper, wrong side up. Following the manufacturer's instructions, spray the wrong side of the fabric piece with adhesive. Place the fabric piece, adhesive side down, onto the background fabric in the appropriate position. Repeat for the remaining pieces. If

desired, use straight pins to hold the pieces down more securely.

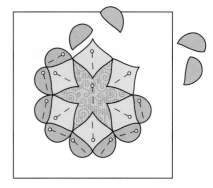

STITCHING THE APPLIQUÉS

If you will not be covering the edges of the appliqués with bias tape, you need to stitch the edges to secure them. Choose a straight machine stitch, a satin stitch or blanket stitch, or your own favorite stitching method. When stitching before layering, place a stabilizer on the wrong side of the fabric to prevent puckering and improve the appearance of the appliqué. I like to use Totally Stable, an iron-on tear-away interfacing made by Sulky, but any tear-away stabilizer is fine. If it's not fusible, pin it to the wrong side of your background fabric so it doesn't shift. If your machine has the needle-down feature, use it for appliqué.

Satin stitch. Set the machine for a narrow, tight zigzag. For most of the small designs, I stitched at a 2.0 mm width, tapering to 1.0 mm at corners and then increasing back to 2.0 mm after the corner is turned. One edge of the zigzag is at the raw edge of the appliqué and the other is on the appliqué.

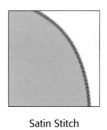

Satin Stitch

Blanket stitch. This stitch gives a hand-stitched look without the hand stitching. Run the vertical stitch along the outside edge of the appliqué and the horizontal stitch on the appliqué. On a small design, use a 2.0 mm width and a 2.0 mm length.

Blanket Stitch

Adding Block Border Designs

Several of the projects include borders to frame and accent the seasonal designs. Think of these as a sort of "mat" around the central motif, as when you frame a piece of artwork.

1. Follow the specific project instructions and trace the border onto paper. Add ¼" to all outside edges. Cut out the shape and use it as a template to cut your chosen fabric. Refer to "Adding Appliqués" on page 13 and follow the directions for your preferred appliqué method. The border appliqué is then ready to be applied to the background fabric. If you are making one block, cut four border units and apply to the background, matching the drawn lines on the background fabric.

¼" added for
seam allowance

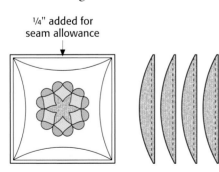

2. When several blocks are joined as in "Hearts and Flowers Table Runner" on page 69, cut the adjoining edge designs as one piece. Simply make two copies of the border design without the ¼" seam allowance and tape the outside edges together. Use that as your pattern to make one unit. The non-adjoining borders will be cut as in step 1.

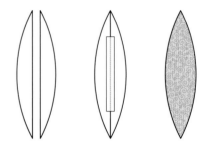

3. Follow the layering instructions in "Assembling the Layers" on page 17. Apply fusible-bias tape over the raw edges of the designs and stitch.

No seam allowance
added

Seam allowance
added to
outside edges

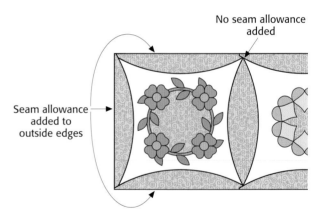

ONE-PIECE BORDERS: MAKE THEM EASY

Before marking and cutting out a one-piece border such as the graceful-curves border on page 94, spray starch the fabric to stabilize it and help control the edges after cutting. If you plan to use fusible web, trace the border onto the paper side of it. Cut ½" away outside the first line, and then cut inside the drawn lines. Adhere just the narrow strip of fusible web to the wrong side of your fabric and cut away the interior part of the fabric on the drawn line. Remove the paper backing and fuse the border to the background.

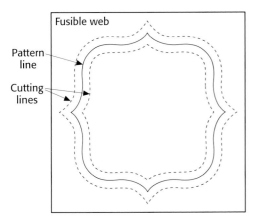

Trim away ½" on either side
of pattern line.

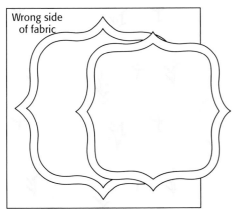

Cut away interior of fabric
on pattern line.

Assembling the Layers

For many of the projects, the next step is to prepare the project for quilting by assembling the top, batting, and backing layers. This will seem out of sequence for those who are familiar with traditional quilting. For most of these Quick Bias projects, you can machine stitch the bias strips in place and do the quilting at the same time. What a time-saver!

There are some exceptions to this sequence, however, so be sure to follow the individual project instructions. Be aware that if you choose to hand stitch the bias tape in place after fusing, you will definitely want to do the stitching before you do the layering, to avoid working with the additional bulk. Unless otherwise stated, the instructions are written for machine stitching, so make changes accordingly for hand stitching. You should also note that the outer borders are added after the project is layered. See "Adding Borders" on page 22 for more specific border instructions.

To assemble the layers, follow the steps below.

1. Lay the backing, wrong side up, on a flat work surface. Smooth out any wrinkles and secure it to the work surface by applying masking tape around all of the edges. Apply the tape to two opposite sides first, then to the remaining two sides, and finally to the corners. Continue arranging the tape until the backing is smooth and taut.

2. Place the batting over the backing and smooth out any wrinkles.

3. Center the background fabric right side up over the batting. Smooth out any wrinkles. Since the borders are often added to the quilt top later, do not be alarmed if there is an excess margin of batting and backing around the top; do not trim it away.

4. Pin baste the layers together with size 1 rust-proof safety pins. Avoid placing pins in areas where the bias tape will be applied.

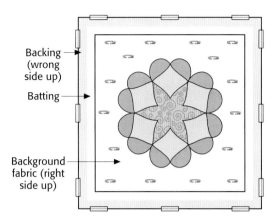

Backing (wrong side up)

Batting

Background fabric (right side up)

Applying the Bias Tape

Now it's time to apply the bias tape to the design lines. Each piece will be fused in place first and then stitched down by hand or machine before the next piece is added, unless otherwise noted.

1. If working with cotton bias tape, set the iron on a cotton setting (high setting on the mini-iron). Use a slightly cooler temperature for metallic bias tape. If using a conventional iron, do not use steam.

QUICK TIP

Before working on your project, do a trial to be sure the iron temperature is correct. Fuse a small piece of bias tape to a scrap of background fabric. It takes just a few seconds to fuse the tape. If the iron is too hot, it will dissolve the adhesive completely. If the iron isn't hot enough, it will not stick at all. Adjust the temperature and pressing time if necessary.

---

2. Refer to the project instructions for the specific sequence in which to apply the tape. If you are working with your own design, plan the sequence so that the ends of each strip are covered by other strips, or make sure that they extend beyond the background fabric and will be enclosed in a border or binding seam. This is extremely important for a clean look. If using a continuous line design, you will use only one strip of tape, beginning and ending at the same point. Plan this point to be at an intersection where another piece will cross over the raw edges and hide them.

Start here.

Tuck under.

Continuous-Line Design

In some instances, such as a circle or the arched-corner border, you need to turn under one edge of the tape and overlap it with the other end. You may need to trim the corners of the end to be tucked under if it shows beneath the remaining strip.

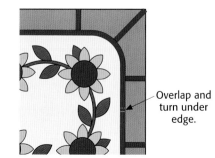

Overlap and turn under edge.

3. Place the project on a portable pressing surface if you have one. Peel off approximately the first 12" of the paper backing from the bias tape. (The backing will not adhere again to the tape once it is removed, so remove the backing only as you work.) With the tape end at the determined beginning point, center the bias tape over the design line. Be sure to place the tape end so it will be completely covered by the strip crossing over it. If two pieces of fabric are butted together covering the design line, center the tape over the butted edges.

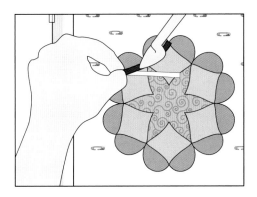

4. Fuse the first piece of bias tape into place, following the correct sequence for your project. Hold the iron in your dominant hand and the tape in the other. If you are right-handed, begin at the starting point and work toward the left of the project. If you are left-handed, work toward the right of the project. Remove the paper backing as you go, and be careful not to stretch the tape as you apply it. Turn the pressing surface as needed to keep the work area in front of you.

5. You will need to either miter or overlap the bias tape at the corners. For angles 90° or greater, miter the tape as directed in step 6. For angles less than 90°, overlap the tape, following the directions in step 7.

6. For a mitered corner, apply bias tape up to the point of the angle. Place the tip of a stiletto over the tape at the point of the angle as shown. Turn the tape to begin applying the next side, but do not press it into place yet. Slowly turn the stiletto tip toward the unpressed tape, stopping when a miter is formed. Press the mitered corner and the next edge in place.

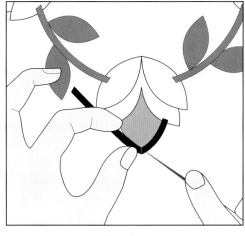

Mitered Corner

7. For an overlapped corner, apply bias tape up to the point of the angle. Place the stiletto tip over the tape at the point of the angle as shown on page 20. Turn the tape to begin applying the next side, but do not press it into place yet. Slowly turn the stiletto tip toward the unpressed edge so that the tape folds over the tip.

Bring the fold to the outer edge of the previously pressed-down edge, and press it into place.

Overlapped Corner

QUICK TIP

Check the fused tape for any mistakes in following the design. If you find an area that needs to be redone, place the iron over the area to loosen the adhesive. Then lift the bias tape up, reposition it, and press it back in place. The adhesive will lose some bonding power each time it is moved, so be careful not to loosen the same area more than absolutely necessary.

8. Stitch the bias tape to the project, using one of the options described in "Stitch Options" on page 21. Begin and end the line of stitching with tiny stitches to lock them in place.

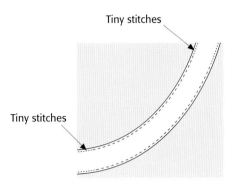

Tiny stitches

Tiny stitches

9. Continue fusing and stitching the bias tape to the design lines until the design is complete.

QUICK TIP

When applying the bias tape to long, straight edges, use a rotary ruler as a guide. Place the ruler edge parallel to the straight edge of the design, leaving enough room to center the tape over the line. Place the edge of the tape parallel to the ruler and guide the iron along it. Being able to see through the ruler will help you keep lines parallel.

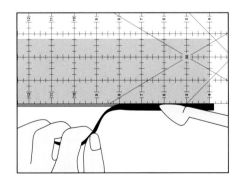

Stitch Options

Stitching the fused bias strips makes them extra secure and ensures that your project will be washable if needed. Use the needle-down feature if your machine has one. Although you can use a standard straight-stitch presser foot, you may find it difficult to see where you are stitching. An open-toe foot allows a clear field of vision. An edge-joining foot works well because the guide runs along the edge of the tape to help stitch accurately. Set the needle so it stitches along the edge of the tape. There are several options for stitching the bias tape down.

Straight-Stitch Foot   Open-Toe Foot

Edge-Joining Foot

TOPSTITCH

Set the machine for a short stitch length, approximately 12 to 15 stitches per inch. This enables you to stitch more effectively and accurately on curves. A slow machine speed will also increase accuracy. Use the needle-down feature and stitch as close to the edge of the tape as possible. When one side of the tape is secure, stitch the other side by moving the needle position or by turning the project around. If your design is made up of straight and/or very gently curving lines, you can also use a double needle to stitch both edges at once. Use a 4.0/90

double needle for the Quick Bias and a 3.0/90 for the Mini Bias.

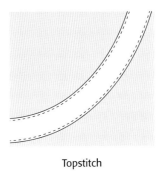

Topstitch

BLIND HEM STITCH

For a hand-stitched look accomplished by machine, use the blind hem stitch. Position the needle so that the straight part of the stitch runs along the outside edge of the tape and the "bite" catches just a couple of threads of tape. Stitch one side of the tape, and then turn the project and stitch the other side, or use the mirror-image feature on your machine if available.

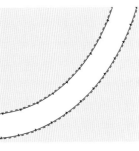

Blind Hem Stitch

DECORATIVE STITCH

One of the decorative stitches on your sewing machine can secure the tape quickly and add textural interest to the project. The featherstitch works well, but feel free to play with some of the other options. Avoid stitches that are created with a lot of back and forth motion, because that causes too much stress on the bias tape. Decorative stitches can be attractive with metallic thread on metallic bias. Or use a contrasting thread color so that the decorative stitch becomes part of the design and enhances your project. Experiment with stitch width to find one that will cover the entire width of the tape in one pass instead of two. You can even extend the stitches beyond the width of the tape as in the snowflake tree skirt. The finished result looks like picot edge ribbon and gives a lacy effect to the snowflake.

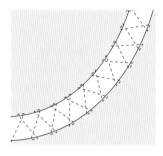

Decorative Stitch

HAND STITCH

The bias tape can also be permanently secured with a hand-appliqué stitch after fusing. Any hand stitching should be done before the project is layered with batting and backing. Choose this method if you prefer handwork or if you are intimidated by machine stitching close to the edge of the tape. The great advantage of hand stitching is that it enables you to control both the stitching and bias tape. The tape responds well to slight easing as you negotiate tight curves. Use an appliqué needle and thread that matches the color of the tape. Use tiny, hidden stitches for a beautifully flat and smooth finish that gives a free-floating, three-dimensional look to your finished project. When you are finished stitching down the tape, layer the top with batting and backing as described in "Assembling the Layers" on page 17. Hand or machine quilt as desired to secure the layers.

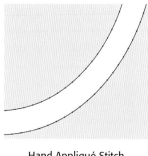

Hand Appliqué Stitch

Adding Borders

Borders are added to most of the projects in this book after the interior of the quilt is quilted, which is a variation on the traditional method.

1. Check the quilt top to be sure it is square before adding borders; mark the border lines again if necessary.

2. Measure the quilt top through its vertical center. Cut the side borders to that length and to the width indicated in the project instructions. With right sides together, place the side borders on the quilt top, aligning the edge of the border with the marked lines as shown. Pin and stitch the side borders in place through all of the layers, using a ¼" seam allowance.

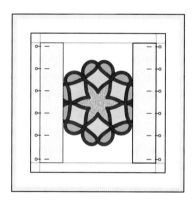

3. Trim the background fabric seam allowance to ¼". Do not trim the batting and backing at this time. From the right side of the quilt top, press the borders out.

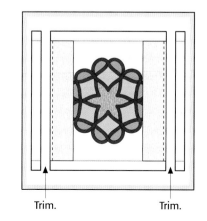

Trim.   Trim.

4. Measure the quilt top through its horizontal center, including the side borders. Cut the top and bottom borders to that length and to the width indicated in the project instructions. Stitch the borders to the top and bottom edges of the quilt in the same manner as the side borders, and trim the seam allowances.

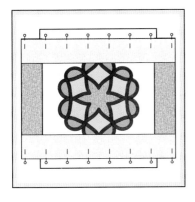

5. Trim the backing and batting even with the edges of the quilt top and finish the borders as indicated in the project instructions. Add additional bias or quilting as desired.

French-Twist Binding

The French-Twist binding is a variation on the commonly used French binding method. By increasing the width of the binding strips to 5" and folding the excess to the back of the quilt, you will easily create two pockets in which to insert a hanging rod. The wider binding also makes the quilt edges more stable and makes the quilt hang better. Use the wide binding technique on wall quilts. For other projects, cut your binding strips 2¼" wide.

1. Join the binding strips into one long, continuous strip using diagonal seams. Trim ¼" from the seam lines and press the seam allowances open.

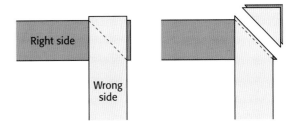

2. Trim one end of the strip at a 45° angle.

3. Fold the binding strip in half lengthwise, wrong sides together, and press.

4. Using straight pins, pin the quilt layers together around the outer edges. Beginning with the angled end, place the binding strip about halfway down one edge of the right side of the quilt. Align the quilt top and binding raw edges. Leaving the first 6" of the binding unstitched, stitch the binding to the quilt. Use a ¼" seam allowance. Stop stitching ¼" from the corner. Backstitch and remove the quilt from the machine.

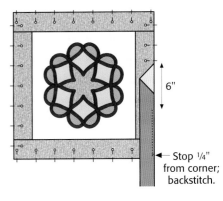

5. Turn the project so you are ready to sew the next side. Fold the binding up so it creates a 45° angle.

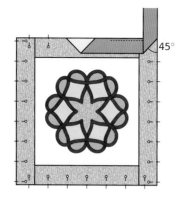

6. Fold the binding back down so the new fold is even with the top edge of the quilt and the binding raw edge is aligned with the side of the quilt. Make sure the binding is relaxed on the quilt; do not pull too tight or the binding will pucker. Beginning at the fold, stitch the binding to the quilt, stopping ¼" from the next corner. Repeat the folding and stitching process for each corner.

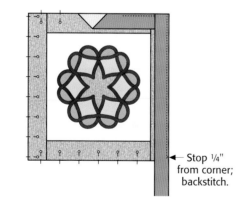

Stop ¼" from corner; backstitch.

7. When you are approximately 6" from the starting point, stop stitching and remove the quilt from the machine. Lay the beginning tail on the quilt top, aligning the raw edges with the quilt top. Lay the ending tail over the beginning tail. Cut the ending tail approximately 2" longer than needed.

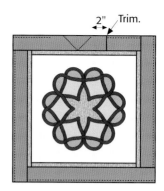

2" Trim.

8. Place the beginning tail inside the ending tail. Make two marks on the ending tail to indicate the angled edges of the beginning tail.

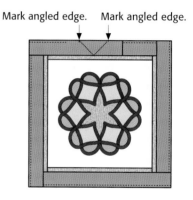

Mark angled edge.   Mark angled edge.

9. Remove the beginning tail from the ending tail. Open up the ending tail so it lies flat with the wrong side up. Mark a diagonal line on the ending tail, connecting the two marked points. Measure ½" to the right of the marked line and mark another line. Trim the excess ending tail along the second marked line.

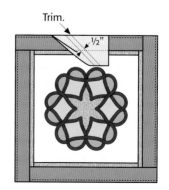

Trim.   ½"

10. Place the beginning and ending tails right sides together with raw edges aligned. Offset the seam so that a small triangle of fabric extends beyond each end as shown. Stitch the ends together, using a ¼" seam allowance. Press the seam allowance open.

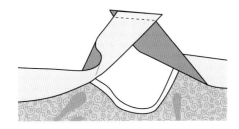

11. Refold the binding. Finish stitching the binding to the edge of the quilt.

12. Remove the straight pins. Press the binding away from the quilt top. Fold the side binding to the back and pin in place.

13. Fold the top and bottom binding to the back and pin in place. Adjust the corners so the binding forms a miter on the front of the quilt and overlaps on the back of the quilt.

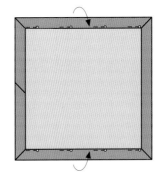

14. For wide binding strips, stitch in the ditch along the binding seam line from the front of the quilt. For narrow binding, slip stitch the binding to the back of the quilt, just covering the machine stitching.

15. From the quilt back, slipstitch the wide binding to the quilt backing along the fold. Do not stitch down the corners for rod pockets. This automatically creates a rod pocket at the top and bottom edges of your quilt.

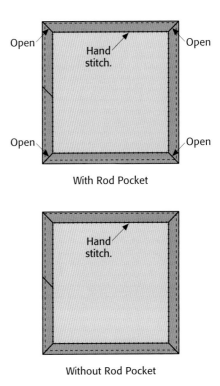

Designing Your Own Seasonal Quilts

YOU CAN CREATE an almost infinite number of projects from the variety of seasonal designs in this book. You can include appliqué with any of the designs, but several can also be made simply with bias tape fused on the background fabric. Some of the appliqué blocks include Mini Bias as a decorative accent or an additional element of the designs. Most of the designs in the book are square or in a wreath format. The smaller patterns are approximately 3" square, designed to be used in a 4"-square background. The wreath patterns are for a 12"-square background. You can enlarge or reduce any of the patterns as desired. The following examples show the variety of projects that can be made with a single appliqué design.

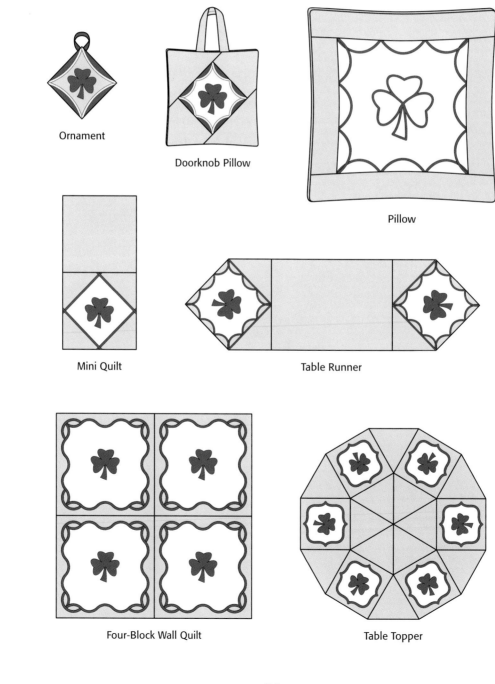

Ornament

Doorknob Pillow

Pillow

Mini Quilt

Table Runner

Four-Block Wall Quilt

Table Topper

Select the Mini Bias for the small designs when used at their actual size; use either the Mini Bias or Quick Bias if the pattern is enlarged (depending on size). When using bias tape with an appliqué pattern, the finished size will be slightly larger than the appliqué. You may have to slightly adjust the percentage for reducing or enlarging to accommodate the size of the bias. See "Enlarging and Reducing the Designs" on page 29 for further directions. I've included charts within that section for adjusting the size of the designs to achieve a specific desired block size.

The star in the middle of each pattern is for ensuring accurate placement onto your chosen block or background. Match the star with the center of the background as instructed in "Transferring the Design" on page 11. The designs can be used either straight or on point.

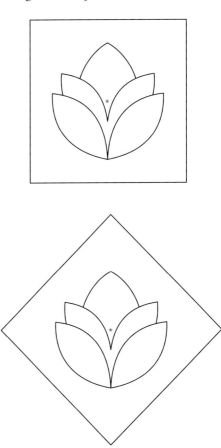

Star indicates center of pattern.

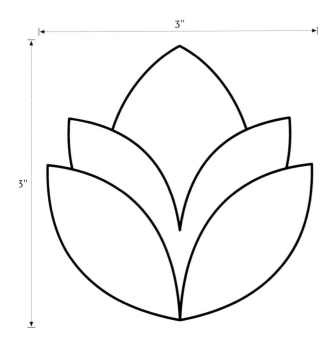

Varying the Block Borders

Create your own designs or further customize any seasonal project by adding border variations. I've included six designs to incorporate into the blocks as desired, beginning on page 91. Three border designs match the 4"-block designs, and three match the 12" designs. Seam allowances are not included because these designs can be used in any size by enlarging or reducing. Once you decide on the size, enlarge or reduce it and then add a ¼" seam allowance to all of the outer edges of the block. Appliqué the fabric to the block edges by simply using the bias tape to stitch the edges down. You can also use the bias tape alone to form the decorative edge. The options are endless.

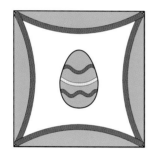

**Fabric Added in Border with
Bias Tape at Raw Edge**

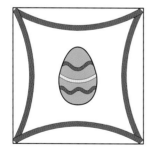

**Just Bias Tape
Covering Border Line**

Adding Corner Triangles

The 4" blocks are the basis for the ornaments, but you can use these designs in many other ways. By adding simple corner triangles and borders of different sizes, you can create a door pillow or mini quilt. The same 4" blocks can be the basis for a wall quilt in which a simple 4" grid is drawn and fusible-bias tape creates the grid lines. See "Patriotic Wall Quilt" on page 56, and "St. Patrick's Day Wall Quilt" on page 60. Any of the block designs can fill the 4" squares inside the grid.

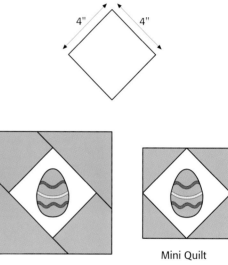

Door Pillow

Mini Quilt

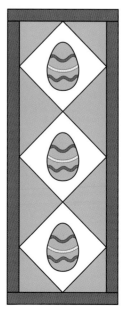

Wall Quilt

Enlarging and Reducing the Designs

THE LARGER YOU make your blocks, the more complex the design elements can be. Make a sample of your seasonal design with different edge treatments to see which border best enhances the design. To test design possibilities, use a photocopier to enlarge or reduce both the seasonal design and border to the desired finished size. Lay the seasonal design under the border design; look at them either on a light box or held up to a light source. Rotate the design to determine if you want it to be on point or straight.

QUICK TIP

Repeat the preceeding test, just prior to starting your project. Hold the designs up to the light to make sure the design looks the way you want and is in pleasing proportions.

Enlarging a 4"-Block Design

1. Choose the desired design. As an example, I will use the single-curve border and the heart appliqué. Let's say that the finished project is going to be 6" square. Refer to the chart on page 30. For a 6" block, enlarge both the single curve and the heart appliqué design by 150%.

2. Add ¼" to all outer edges of the single-curve border.

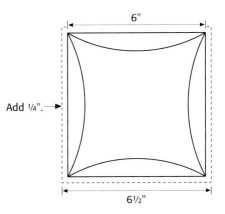

♦ 29 ♦

3. Cut the square of background fabric 6½" x 6½" since the ¼" seam allowance is added to all sides for the enlarged design.

ENLARGING THE 4" DESIGNS

Enlarge both the appliqué designs and the border designs by the same percentage.

Desired Block Size	Enlargement
4"	100%
5"	125%
6"	150%
7"	175%
8"	200%
9"	225%
10"	250%
11"	275%
12"	300%

Reducing a 12"-Block Design

1. Choose the desired design. As an example, I will use the graceful-curves border and the posy wreath. Let's assume that I want a block that finishes at 10" square. Refer to the chart at right. For a 10" block, reduce both the curves and the wreath by 84% on a photocopy machine. Work with the quadrant given on page 94 and make four reduced copies.

2. Tape the copies together, matching overlay lines. Add ¼" to all outside edges of the graceful-curves border.

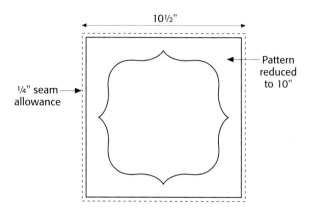

3. Cut a 10½" x 10½" square of background fabric since the ¼" seam allowances are added on all sides of the reduced design.

REDUCING THE 12" DESIGNS

Reduce both the wreath designs and the border designs by the same percentage.

Desired Block Size	Reduction
12"	100%
11"	92%
10"	84%
9"	75%
8"	67%
7"	58%
6"	50%

Reducing and Enlarging

You can mix and match smaller designs with larger designs for even more possibilities. An example would be the 12" arched-corner border and the 4" leaf shape. Let's say that you want an 8" finished block. Refer to the chart below. The border would be reduced by 67% and the leaf appliqué would be enlarged by 156%. Cut a square that is 8½" x 8½" from both the background and border fabrics.

REDUCING 12" DESIGNS AND ENLARGING 4" DESIGNS

Desired Block Size	Reduction 12" Border or Wreath Designs	Enlargement 4" Designs
12"	100%	248%
11"	92%	225%
10"	84%	202%
9"	75%	180%
8"	67%	156%
7"	58%	134%
6"	50%	113%

ORNAMENTS

These ornaments can be stitched together quickly to add a decorative touch for any holiday, not just Christmas. Even Groundhog Day deserves a tree! They could also be festive gift tags, or eliminate the ribbon and you have holiday coasters.

Basic Ornament

Finished ornament: 4" x 4"

Celtic Rose

Snowflake 1

Snowflake 2

Snowflake 3

Materials

(for one ornament)

♦ 1 fat eighth of a solid or subtle print for background and backing

♦ 1 yard of Mini Bias

♦ 4½" x 4½" piece of thin batting or fleece

♦ Sew-through fusible web

♦ 5" piece of ribbon for hanger

Cutting

All measurements include ¼"-wide seam allowance.

From the solid or subtle print, cut:

♦ 2 squares, 4½" x 4½"

♦ 1 square, 2¼" x 2¼"

Construction

1. Select a design from the appliqué and bias design patterns on page 83. Refer to "Transferring the Design" on page 11 and trace the chosen design onto the 4½" background square.

2. Layer the background square on the 4½" square of batting. Pin baste around the edges, keeping pins out of the way of the design. Fuse the appliqué and/or Mini Bias.

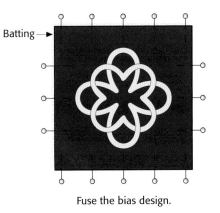

Batting →

Fuse the bias design.

3. Stitch the appliqué or Mini Bias design using one of the stitch options on page 21.

4. Fold the ribbon in half and pin it to one corner or center it on one side. The raw edges should be even with the edge of the block as shown. For a corner hanger, keep the ribbon ends ¼" away on each side of the corner to eliminate bulk.

Center Hanger

Corner Hanger

5. Layer the 4½" backing square, right sides together, with the ornament front. Pin. Stitch all the way around the square, starting in the middle of one side. At the corners, stitch one stitch on an angle as shown, instead of pivoting 90°. This will make sharper corners.

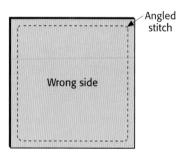

Angled stitch

Wrong side

6. Grade the seam allowances at the corners by cutting off the point and angling the sides.

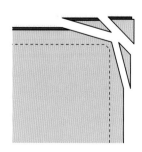

Trim corners.

7. Carefully lift the backing fabric away from the front so you can cut a small + in the backing, about 1½" long. Do not cut the ribbon hanger. Turn the ornament inside out through the opening. Push out the corners using a point turner or blunt instrument, such as a knitting needle. (Do not use scissors; the points are too sharp.) Press.

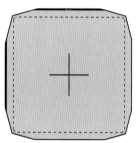

8. Apply fusible web to the 2¼" square of backing fabric. Trim to 2" square. Press over the opening on the back of the ornament to close it up.

QUICK TIP

Use a light, contrasting fabric for the 2" square that conceals the opening. Sign your name and the date or write "To:" and "From:" to use the ornament as a gift tag.

Nine Patch Ornament

Finished ornament: 4" x 4"

Materials

- 1 fat eighth of print for background and backing
- 1½" x 8½" piece of red for accent
- 1 yard of Mini Bias
- 4½" x 4½" piece of thin batting or fleece
- Sew-through fusible web
- 5" piece of ribbon for hanger

Cutting

All measurements include ¼"-wide seam allowance.

From the print, cut:
- 2 squares, 4½" x 4½"
- 1 square, 2¼" x 2¼"

Construction

1. Draw a line 1¼" in from all the sides of the 4½" background square.

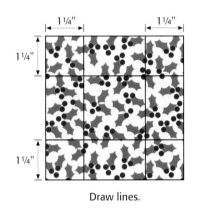

Draw lines.

2. Apply the fusible web to the wrong side of the accent fabric. Cut it into four pieces, 1¼" x 2". Remove the paper backing.

3. Position the accent pieces on the background square, making sure that the corners of the rectangles meet precisely at the intersections. Fuse.

Meet precisely.

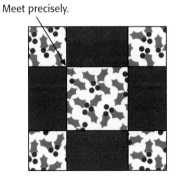

4. Layer the background square on the 4½" square of batting. Pin baste around the edges.

5. Apply Mini Bias, centering it over the raw edges of the fused pieces, from raw edge to raw edge. Stitch in place using your preferred method as described on page 21.

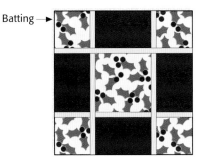

Batting →

Apply Mini Bias.

6. Follow steps 4–8 on page 34 of the instructions for "Basic Ornament" to complete your ornament.

Square-in-a-Square Ornament

Finished ornament: 4" x 4"

Materials

- 1 fat eighth of print for background and backing
- Scrap of red for accent
- Scrap of green for accent
- 1 yard of Mini Bias
- 4½" x 4½" piece of thin batting or fleece
- Sew-through fusible web
- 5" piece of ribbon for hanger

Cutting

All measurements include ¼"-wide seam allowance.

From the print, cut:
- 2 squares, 4½" x 4½"
- 1 square, 2¼" x 2¼"

From the red accent, cut:
- 1 square, 3" x 3"

From the green accent, cut:
- 1 square, 2¼" x 2¼"

Construction

1. Fold the background square in half twice to create quarters; press lightly.

2. Adhere fusible web to the wrong side of the red accent and green accent squares. Trim the red square to 2⅞" x 2⅞" and the green square to 2" x 2".

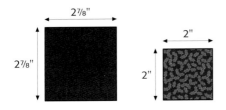

3. Position the red accent square on the 4½" background square as shown. Use the creases to assist in centering and aligning. Fuse the red square. Center the green accent square over the red square. All four corners of the green should touch the midpoints of the sides of the red square. Fuse in place.

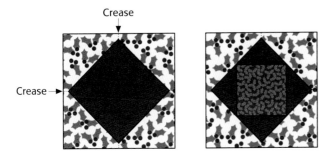

4. Layer the background square on the 4½" square of batting. Pin baste around the edges.

5. Apply Mini Bias along the edges of the center square. Stitch in place using your preferred method on page 21. Apply Mini Bias along the edges of the larger square. Stitch in place.

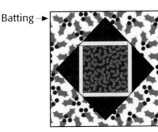

6. Follow steps 4–8 on page 34 of the instructions for "Basic Ornament" to complete your ornament.

QUICK TIP

Cut any fabric that will be fused onto your ornaments oversized. Adhere the fusible web and then trim it to the needed size and shape. That way you know that the piece is fully covered with the fusible web.

Medallion Ornament

Finished ornament: 4" x 4"

Materials

- 1 fat eighth of solid fabric for background and backing
- Scrap of print fabric for corner triangles
- 1 yard of Mini Bias
- 4½" x 4½" piece of thin batting or fleece
- Sew-through fusible web
- 5" piece of ribbon for hanger

Cutting

All measurements include ¼"-wide seam allowance.

From the solid, cut:

- 2 squares, 4½" x 4½"
- 1 square, 2¼" x 2¼"

From the print, cut:

- 2 squares, 3" x 3"

Construction

1. Trace the chosen design (medallion on page 86) and block border onto one of the 4½" solid squares.

2. Apply fusible web to the wrong side of the two 3" print squares. Trim the squares to 2½". Cut diagonally once to form four triangles.

3. Position and fuse the triangles to the 4½" solid square, matching the drawn lines.

4. Layer the square from step 3 on the 4½" square of batting. Pin baste around the edges.

5. Apply Mini Bias to the center design. Stitch in place using your preferred method on page 21. Apply Mini Bias to the long edges of the corner triangles. Stitch in place.

Batting→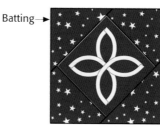

6. Follow steps 4–8 on page 34 of the instructions for "Basic Ornament" to complete your medallion ornament.

DOORKNOB PILLOWS

Dress up those lonely doorknobs for the holidays with these little puffy pillows. Think of those spaces where you want to add something festive, but space is limited. Follow the instructions for "Easter Egg Doorknob Pillow," and vary the designs to suit your favorite season or holiday.

Easter Egg Doorknob Pillow

Finished pillow: 7½" x 7½" ◆ *Finished block: 4" x 4"*

Materials

- 1 fat quarter of seasonal print for corner triangles, hanger, and backing
- 5" x 5" piece of cream for block background
- Scraps for appliqué and block border
- 1 yard of Mini Bias
- 8" x 8" piece of thin batting or fleece
- 2 to 4 ounces of fiberfill
- Fusible web

Cutting

All measurements include ¼"-wide seam allowance.

From the cream background, cut:

- 1 square, 4½" x 4½"

From the seasonal print, cut:

- 2 squares, 6" x 6"; cut diagonally once to create 4 triangles
- 1 square, 8" x 8"
- 1 piece, 2" x 8"

Construction

1. Trace the chosen border design (single curve on page 91) onto the 4½" background square, referring to "Transferring the Design" on page 11. Trace the appliqué (egg on page 84) onto the fusible web.

2. Prepare the border pieces and appliqués. Apply and fuse them to the background. Add the Mini Bias to cover the raw edges of the border and create designs on the appliqué, if desired. Do not stitch yet.

3. Fold the batting in half twice to mark the quarters; lightly press. Center the square, on point, onto the batting. The corners of the square should meet the creases in the batting.

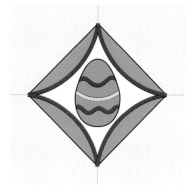

4. Stitch the appliqués and bias border designs using your preferred stitch. Refer to "Stitching the Appliqués" on page 15 and "Stitch Options" on page 21.

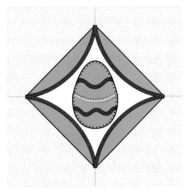

5. Add the corner triangles as shown. Sew two opposite sides on first; press toward the triangles. Sew the remaining sides, trim the excess, and press.

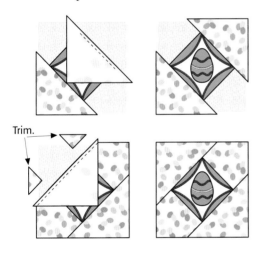

Trim.

6. Trim the block to 8" square. Mark 3" in from each corner along the top edge.

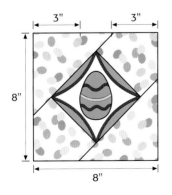

3"   3"

8"

8"

7. Fold the 2" x 8" piece of print fabric lengthwise, right sides together. Stitch a ¼" seam along the length and turn right side out for the hanger. Press, centering the seam on the back of the hanger. Position and pin the hanger at the marks on the top of the square.

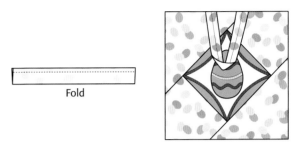

Fold

8. Layer the 8" square of backing, right sides together, with the completed front. Stitch around the outside edge, leaving an opening on the center of the bottom edge for turning. Instead of pivoting 90° at the corners, angle stitch one stitch to create a sharper corner.

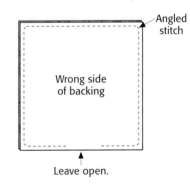

Angled stitch

Wrong side of backing

Leave open.

9. Grade the corners, turn right side out, and press. Stuff with fiberfill to the desired fullness and stitch the opening closed.

Stitch closed.

TWO-IN-ONE MINI QUILTS

I first saw a mini quilt rack at a craft show, and I loved the idea of making small quilts to display on these decorative hangers or to give as gifts. Each quilt is reversible, so you will need to make two different blocks to complete one quilt.

Snowflake and Flower Mini Quilt

Each side features a different 4" block design.

Finished mini quilt: 6" x 12" ◆ Finished block: 4" x 4"

Materials

Note: You will need the following quantities for each side of the mini quilt.

- ◆ 1 fat quarter of seasonal print for corner triangles and backing
- ◆ 5" x 5" scrap of cream for block background
- ◆ Scraps for appliqués
- ◆ 1 yard of Mini Bias
- ◆ 8" x 8" piece of thin batting or fleece
- ◆ Fusible web

Cutting

All measurements include ¼"-wide seam allowance. For each side of the quilt, cut the following:

From the cream background, cut:

- ◆ 1 square, 4½" x 4½"

From the seasonal print, cut:

- ◆ 2 squares, 6" x 6"; cut diagonally once to create 4 triangles
- ◆ 1 square, 6½" x 6½"
- ◆ 1 square, 2¼" x 2¼"

Construction

1. Trace snowflake 1 (page 00) on to the 4½" background square.

2. Apply Mini Bias to the drawn design.

3. Fold the batting in half twice to mark the quarters; lightly press. Center the square, on point, onto the batting. The corners of the square should meet the creases in the batting.

4. Stitch the snowflake.

5. Add the corner triangles. Sew two opposite sides on first; press toward the tri-angles. Sew the remaining sides, trim, and press.

6. Add Mini Bias along the seam after the corner triangles are in place.

7. Trim the block to 6½" square.

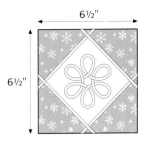

8. Repeat for the reverse side, tracing the sunflower design (page 85) onto fusible web. Adhere the fusible web to the appliqué fabrics and fuse in place on the background square. Mark a line ⅝" from the outer edges of the block along all sides; apply bias tape along each line.

9. Layer the block with the batting; stitch and then add the corner triangles as before. Trim the block to 6½" square.

10. Stitch the 6½" seasonal-print square to the completed block along the top edge. Press toward the print square. Repeat with the second block.

11. Place the completed units right sides together, positioned so that each design square faces a plain square. Stitch around the quilts using a ¼" seam allowance. Instead of pivoting 90° at the corners, angle stitch one stitch to create a sharper corner. Grade the corners.

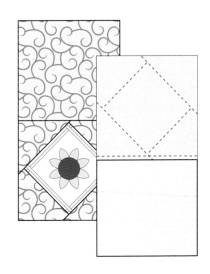

12. Carefully lift the backing of one of the quilts away from the front so you can cut a small + without catching the front of the quilt.

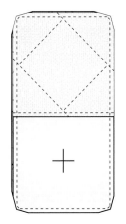

13. Turn the quilt right side out. Push out the corners using a blunt instrument. Press. Pin baste with safety pins.

14. Apply fusible web to the 2¼" square of fabric that matches the fabric with the opening. Trim to 2" square. Press over the cut on the back of the quilt to conceal the opening.

15. Quilt as desired.

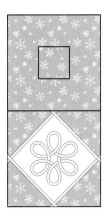

DESIGN OPTIONS

Instead of using a 4" block on point and adding corner triangles, add a 1½" border (1" finished size) on all sides to create a 6" finished block. You can also simply use a 6" finished block design.

Star and Basket Mini Quilt

This side of the mini quilt features a 4" block design with a double-curved border. Add a 1½" border to create a 6" finished block.

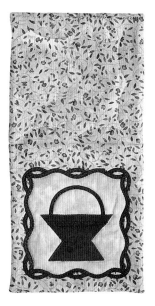

The reverse side features the 6" basket appliqué with the wave border.

DOOR DECORATIONS

Adding a holiday decoration to your front door sets a welcoming and festive tone for guests arriving at your home. Door decorations are also perfect for apartment dwellers who have limited wall space and want to personalize their entryway.

Spring Basket Door Decoration

Finished decoration: 9½" x 9½" ◆ *Finished block: 9" x 9"*

Materials

All yardages are based on 42"-wide fabric.

◆ 1 fat quarter of seasonal print for block border and binding
◆ ⅜ yard of white print for background and backing
◆ Scraps of fabrics for appliqué
◆ 2 yards of Quick Bias
◆ 11" x 11" piece of lightweight batting

Cutting

All measurements include ¼"-wide seam allowance.

From the white print, cut:
◆ 1 square, 9½" x 9½"
◆ 1 square, 11" x 11"

From the seasonal print, cut:
◆ 2 strips, 2¼" x 22"

QUICK TIP

This project uses the ¼" Quick Bias, but you could use two parallel rows of Mini Bias instead to create a different look.

Construction

1. Enlarge or reduce the chosen border design (graceful curves on page 94) and seasonal design (basket appliqué on page 86) to fit a 9" block. Refer to "Enlarging and Reducing the Designs" on page 29.

2. Trace the designs onto the 9½" background square, referring to "Transferring the Design" on page 11.

3. Prepare and fuse the appliqué or bias designs and the border fabric. Refer to "Adding Appliqués" on page 13 as needed.

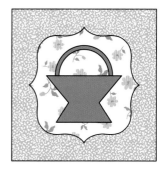

◆ 47 ◆

4. Layer with backing and batting.

5. Apply and fuse the bias tape to the raw edge of the border design. Stitch and add additional quilting as desired.

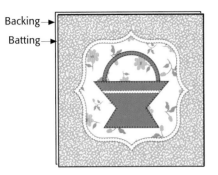

6. Trim the backing and batting even with the raw edge of the completed top.

7. Add 2¼"-wide binding, referring to "French-Twist Binding" on page 23. A café-curtain ring or D ring works well for hanging the decoration on a nail or decorative hook.

DESIGN OPTIONS

For a fall quilt, I used the medallion design enlarged to a 9" block size. I enlarged the pumpkin appliqué pattern on page 85 to fit the 6" opening in the center and added an additional row of variegated bias tape ½" away to frame the center block. Hand sew a café-curtain ring to the back and hang the quilt on point.

Pumpkin Door Decoration

PILLOWS

Pillows always add a bit of warmth and charm to seasonal decor. Combine the wreath and border options in almost unlimited ways to make many creative accessories for your home. "Posy Wreath Pillow" in the photograph has mitered borders, but I've simplified the construction with straight borders.

Posy Wreath Pillow

Finished pillow: 16" x 16" ◆ *Finished block: 12" x 12"*

Materials

All yardages are based on 42"-wide fabric.

- ½ yard of floral print for inner and outer borders
- ½ yard of white for appliqué background and backing of pillow top
- ⅜ yard of mottled blue for piping and flowers
- ¼ yard of green print for bias stems, leaves, and border **or** 1½ yards of green Quick Bias and ⅛ yard of green print for leaves
- Scrap of yellow fabric for flower centers
- ¾ yard of blue print for the envelope back of pillow
- Stabilizer for machine appliqué (For information on stabilizers, refer to "Stitching the Appliqués" on page 15.)
- 18" x 18" piece of lightweight batting
- 16" x 16" pillow form

Cutting

All measurements include ¼"-wide seam allowance.

From the white background, cut:
- 1 square, 14" x 14"
- 1 square, 18" x 18"

From the green print*, cut:
- 6 bias strips, each a generous ½" x 12"

From the mottled blue, cut:
- 9 bias strips, 1" x 18"

From the floral print, cut:
- 1 square, 14" x 14"
- 2 pieces, 2½" x 12½"
- 2 pieces, 2½" x 16½"

*Cut only if you are making your own bias tape. Cut the strips just a few threads wider than ½".

Construction

1. Trace the chosen border design (graceful curves on page 94) and appliqué (posy wreath on page 87) onto the background square, referring to "Transferring the Design" on page 11.

2. To make the project as shown, prepare 12 leaves, four flowers, and four center circles

using your preferred method of appliqué. Refer to "Adding Appliqués" on page 13 as needed, and use a stabilizer on the wrong side of the square behind the appliqué area. Apply bias tape for the wreath first and stitch in place. Add the leaves and stitch. Then add the flowers. Stitch the petal markings and then the outer edges of the flowers. Stitch around the center circle of each flower. After the appliqué is stitched, remove the stabilizer.

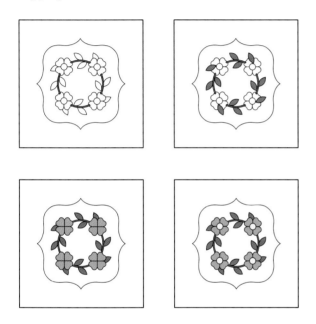

3. Prepare and appliqué the border to the background using the 14" x 14" floral-print square. Apply bias tape to cover the edges. Stitch. Trim and square up the block to 12½" x 12½".

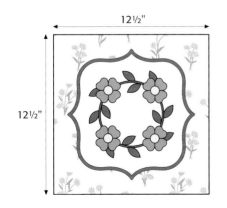

4. Add the decorative scalloped piping. Fold four blue 1" bias strips in half lengthwise, wrong sides together. Press. Set your machine for a blind hem stitch and stitch down the center of the bias strip. The "bite" should catch the folded edge on the left. Practice on scrap fabric first, and adjust the tension and stitch width and length to get the desired effect. I used 6.0 mm width, 2.0 mm length, and an upper tension of 7 (normal is 4.5) on my machine.

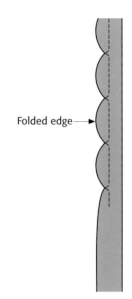

Folded edge ⟶

5. Pin a completed strip of piping to each of the block edges, keeping raw edges even. Baste in place by machine with a scant ¼" seam.

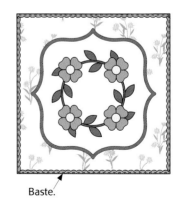

Baste.

6. Add the outer borders, referring to "Adding Borders" on page 22.

7. Layer the appliqué square with the batting and 18" x 18" white backing. Pin baste. Quilt crosshatching in the background around the appliqués and border, or quilt as desired.

8. Trim the batting and backing even with the edges of the pillow top. It should measure 16½" x 16½".

9. Add decorative piping to the outside of the pillow. Stitch the remaining blue 1" bias strips together to form one long strip. Press the seams open and trim seam allowances to ⅛". Follow steps 4 and 5 to create and add the piping. Baste in place with a scant ¼" seam.

Envelope Backing

For pillow tops 16" x 16" or smaller:

1. Stitch a scant ¼" from the outside edges of the pillow top if you did not add piping.

2. To make the envelope backing for the pillow, measure the pillow top through the horizontal center. Add 2" to this measurement; this will be the width to cut the backing. For this pillow, the width should be 18½". Cut a piece of blue print fabric 42" long by the determined width. Cut this piece in half widthwise. Press

each of the pieces in half widthwise, wrong sides together.

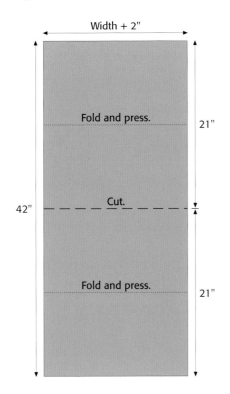

3. With right sides together, pin the pillow back pieces to the pillow top, overlapping the folds in the center of the top by 4". The back pieces will extend beyond the edges of the pillow top. Pin the layers in place.

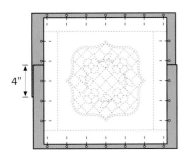

4. Stitch the back pieces to the pillow top, stitching just inside the basting stitches. Stitch the corners at an angle.

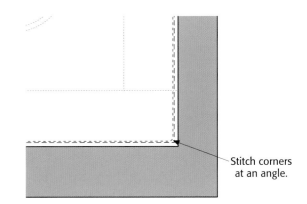

5. Trim the back even with the pillow top. Turn the pillow right side out. Insert the pillow form.

For pillow tops larger than those in this book (16" x 16"):

1. Follow steps 1 and 2 on page 52, but do not fold the two backing pieces in half.

2. With right sides together, place the backing pieces on the pillow top. Arrange the backing pieces so that the pillow top is centered. Fold and arrange the backing pieces so that there is a 4" overlap in the center. Press the folded edges and stitch them in place at the raw edges.

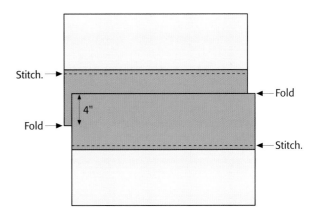

3. Follow steps 3–5 above to finish the pillow cover.

DESIGN OPTIONS

AUTUMN LEAVES

I used four 6" blocks to create a 12" square pillow and added the leaf appliqués on point. I then added a 1" finished outer border and used Mini Bias to highlight the entire design.

Finished size: 14" x 14"

HEARTS ALL AROUND

For this pillow, I wanted a 10" finished background square, so I reduced the heart wreath design and appliquéd it onto the background, accented with the wave border (reduced 84%). I then added a ½" finished inner border and a 1½" finished outer border to make a 14" square pillow.

Finished size: 14" x 14"

WALL QUILTS

These wall quilts celebrate the seasons in a slightly larger format than the previous projects. Hang them on the wall, or use them on a table or on the top of a sideboard. The three-"block" size could also be used on a front door.

Patriotic Wall Quilt

Finished quilt: 10" x 21" ♦ *Finished "block": 4" x 4"*

Materials

All yardages are based on 42"-wide fabric.

- ½ yard of seasonal print for outer border and binding
- 1 fat quarter of white print for background
- ⅛ yard of red print for inner border
- Scraps for appliqués
- 2 yards of Quick Bias **or** 4 yards of Mini Bias
- ½ yard of fabric for backing
- 12" x 23" piece of batting
- Stabilizer for machine appliqué

Cutting

All measurements include ¼"-wide seam allowance.

From the white print, cut:
- 1 piece, 10" x 21"

From the red print, cut:
- 2 strips, 1" x 42"

From the seasonal print, cut:
- 2 strips, 2" x 42"
- 2 strips, 5" x 42"

From the backing, cut:
- 1 piece, 12" x 23"

Construction

1. Fold the background in half lengthwise and widthwise.

2. Mark 2" in on all sides of the background piece to create a temporary outside edge of 6" x 17". Trace the outline of the 4" "block" on

---

QUICK TIP

You can make this quilt with two rows of Mini Bias or one row of Quick Bias. Consider positioning your appliqués so the wall hanging will be horizontal instead of vertical.

point in the center. Then draw the two adjacent 4" squares as shown. Use the grid pattern on page 59 as a guide.

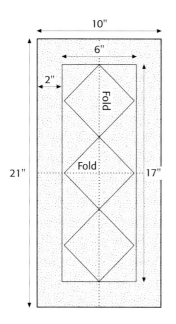

3. Prepare three appliqués of your chosen design (star is on page 84). Position and fuse the appliqué shapes. Machine appliqué using a stabilizer if you will not be finishing the edges of the appliqué with bias tape.

4. If you wish to use two rows of the Mini Bias as I did, instead of one row of the Quick Bias, draw a line ⅛" away on both sides of the marked lines.

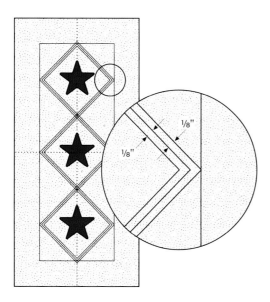

5. Center the background on the batting and backing. Pin baste.

6. Apply bias tape on the marked lines. Use a ruler for accuracy (see page 20). Stitch the bias tape in place after each row is applied. Add additional quilting if desired.

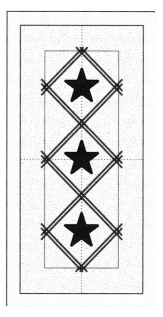

7. Make sure the top is square by measuring from side to side and from corner to corner. Adjust the outer drawn lines if necessary. Using a ruler, mark the top ¼" away from the outer edge of the bias intersections as shown. Trim the excess background fabric only along this line. Do not cut into the batting or backing.

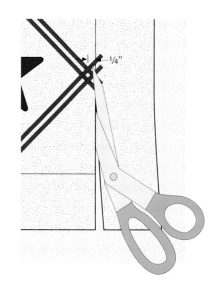

8. Refer to "Adding Borders" on page 22. Cut the 1" x 42" inner borders to the correct length and stitch the inner borders to the quilt top, stitching through all the layers. Repeat to cut and stitch the 2" outer borders to the quilt top.

9. Refer to "French-Twist Binding" on page 23 to bind your quilt.

DESIGN OPTIONS

Make several of these wallhangings in different seasonal prints and give them as a gift. Your gifts can be enjoyed all year long.

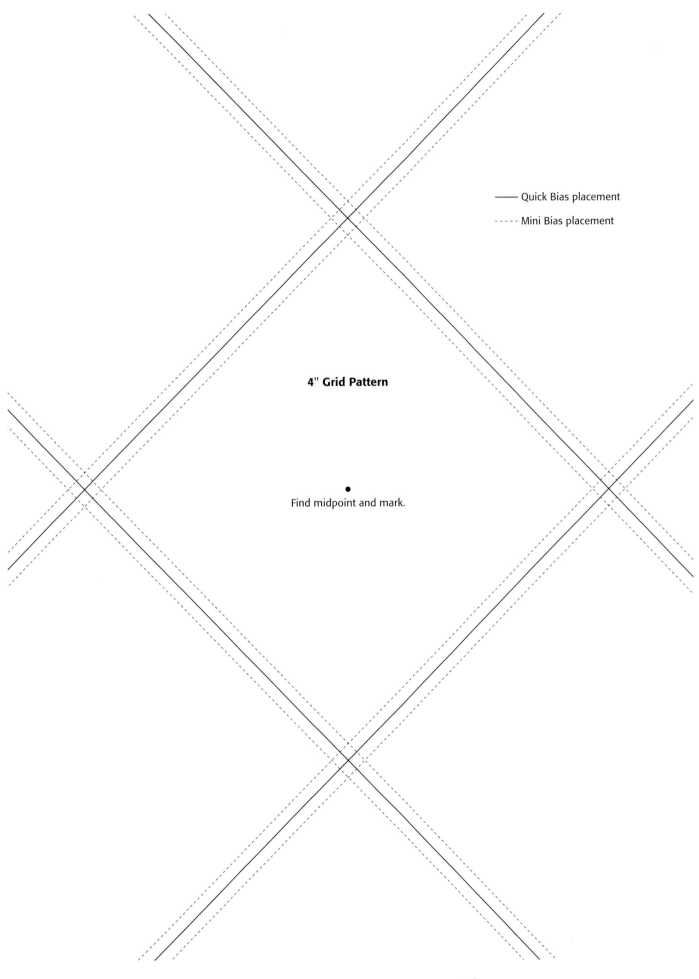

——— Quick Bias placement

- - - - Mini Bias placement

4" Grid Pattern

●

Find midpoint and mark.

St. Patrick's Day Wall Quilt

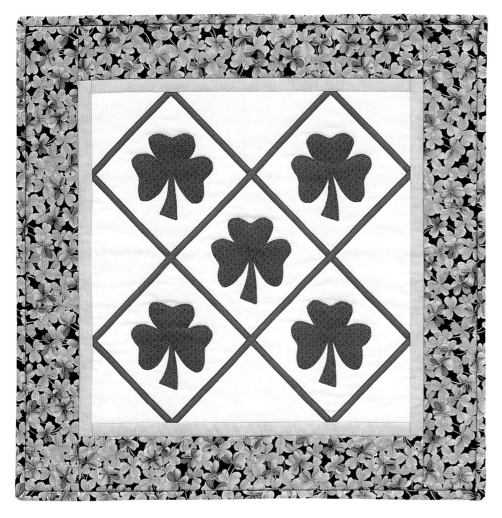

Finished quilt: 17" x 17"   ♦   Finished "block": 4" x 4"

Materials

All yardages are based on 42"-wide fabric.

♦ ⅝ yard of seasonal print for outer border and binding

♦ 1 fat quarter of white for background

♦ ⅛ yard of mint green for inner border

♦ Scraps for appliqués

♦ 2½ yards of Quick Bias **or** 5 yards of Mini Bias

♦ ¾ yard of fabric for backing

♦ 20" x 20" piece of batting

♦ Stabilizer for machine appliqué

Cutting

All measurements include ¼"-wide seam allowance.

From the white, cut:
♦ 1 square, 12½" x 12½"

From the mint green, cut:
♦ 2 strips, 1" x 42"

From the seasonal print, cut:
♦ 2 strips, 2½" x 42"
♦ 2 strips, 5" x 42"

From the backing, cut:
♦ 1 square, 20" x 20"

Construction

1. Fold the background fabric in half twice to mark the quarters; lightly press.

2. Trace the outline of the 4" "block" on page 59 on point, in the center of the background, referring to "Transferring the Design" on page 11. Repeat to draw the remaining four "blocks."

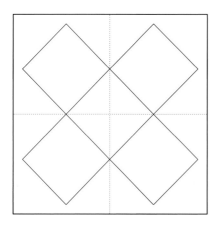

3. Prepare five appliqués of your chosen design (shamrock is on page 84) using your preferred method of appliqué. Position and fuse the appliqué shapes. Machine appliqué using a stabilizer if you will not be finishing the edges of the appliqué with bias tape.

4. Follow steps 4–7 for "Patriotic Wall Quilt" on page 57. Machine quilt around the appliqués as desired.

5. Refer to "Adding Borders" on page 22. Cut the 1" x 42" inner borders to the correct length. Stitch the inner borders to the quilt top. Repeat to cut and stitch the 2½" outer borders to the quilt top.

6. Refer to "French-Twist Binding" on page 23 to bind your quilt.

Tulip Wreath Wall Quilt

Finished quilt: 30" x 30" ◆ *Finished block: 12" x 12"*
Made by Betty Hanneman, 2003, Watertown, Wisconsin. Hand quilted by Mary Kotek.

This project uses the wreath design in a 12" square, but you can adjust the block to any size that you wish. Betty used a creamy batik as the background for these stained-glass tulip wreaths, framed by a softly curving batik-print border.

Materials

All yardages are based on 42"-wide fabric.

- 1½ yards of batik print for curved inner borders, outer border, and binding
- ⅞ yard of creamy yellow for appliqué background
- ⅜ yard of green print for leaves and stems **or** scraps of green for leaves and 1½ yards of green Quick Bias for stems
- Fabric scraps or 1 fat eighth *each* of one light rose and one dark rose for tulips
- 10 yards of black Mini Bias
- 4 yards of black Quick Bias
- 1⅛ yards of fabric for backing
- 32" x 32" piece of batting

Cutting

All measurements include ¼"-wide seam allowance.

From the creamy yellow, cut:
- 4 squares, 12½" x 12½"

From the backing, cut:
- 1 square, 32" x 32"

From the green print*, cut:
- 6 bias strips, each a generous ½" x 12"

From the batik print, cut:
- 4 strips, 3½" x 42"
- 3 strips, 5" x 42"

*Cut bias strips only if you are making your own bias. Cut the strips just a few threads wider than ½".

Construction

1. Fold the background fabric squares into quarters, referring to "Transferring the Design" on page 11.

2. Trace the appliqué and border designs onto the center of the background squares. To make the project as shown, trace the tulip wreath pattern on page 89 and the triple-curve border pattern on page 92 sized for a 12" block.

Trace 4.

3. Stitch the four background squares together and press the seams open.

4. Center the large background square on the batting and backing. Pin baste; keep pins away from the appliqué lines.

5. Prepare the chosen appliqués. To make the quilt like the one in the photograph, you will need: 16 tulip tips, 16 tulip petals, 32 individual leaves, and 16 pairs of leaves for the tulips.

6. Fuse or stitch the shapes to the background using your preferred method of appliqué. Apply bias tape for the wreath first and stitch in place. Add the leaves around the wreath and stitch them. Add the tulip tips; apply and stitch Mini Bias around the tips. Add the tulip petals; apply and stitch Mini Bias around the petals. Then add tulip leaves; apply and stitch Mini Bias around the leaves, starting and stopping in the center so the raw edge is covered.

7. Prepare the border fabric using the batik print. Select your preferred appliqué method, referring to page 13. Cut four double sections and eight single sections of the triple-curve border on page 92.

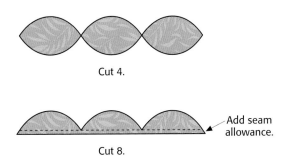

Cut 4.

Add seam allowance.

Cut 8.

8. Position the eight single sections following the traced lines. Fuse. Stitch Mini Bias along the curves, extending the beginning and ending edges of bias into the seam area to be covered when the outer border is attached. Then position the four double sections following the traced lines. Fuse and stitch Mini Bias to the double sections, again extending the beginning and ending edges of the bias tape into the seam area.

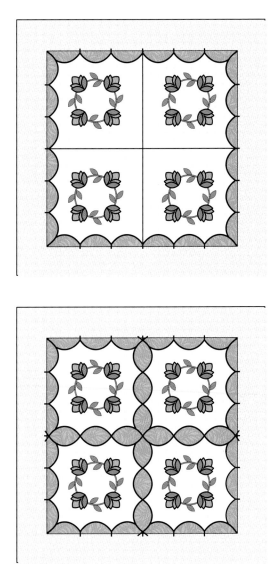

9. Add additional quilting as desired.

10. Refer to "Adding Borders" on page 22 to cut the 3½" outer-border strips to the correct length and add them to the quilt. Stitch the outer borders to the quilt top.

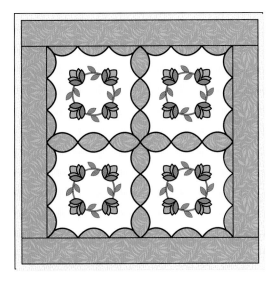

11. Apply Quick Bias to the seam line if desired.

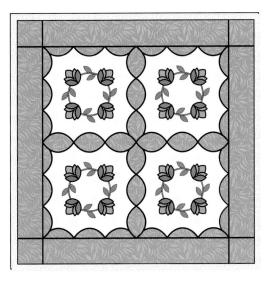

12. Refer to "French-Twist Binding" on page 23 to bind your quilt.

DESIGN OPTIONS

Mix and match border designs with appliqué and bias design patterns for endless variations on this four-block wall quilt.

Pillow with Hearts (page 83) on Point and Single-Curve Border (page 91)

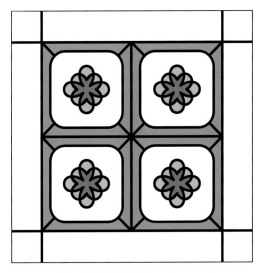

Wall Quilt with Celtic Rose (page 86) and Arched-Corner Border (page 93)

TABLE RUNNERS

The dining room is the center of many holiday gatherings with our family and friends. You can display your handiwork in a seasonal table runner and add to the festivities as well. Choose from two different layouts or make both! Incorporate your favorite designs to make a table runner for every occasion.

Sunflower Wreath Table Runner

Finished quilt: 48" x 14" ◆ Finished block: 10" x 10"

Made by Betty Hanneman, 2003, Watertown, Wisconsin. Hand quilted by Mary Kotek.

The sunflower wreath was appliquéd in the end blocks and repeated as a quilting design in the center to create this fall table runner.

Materials

All yardages are based on 42"-wide fabric.

◆ 1 yard of pale yellow batik for background
◆ ⅝ yard of brown batik for border and binding
◆ 1 fat quarter of green print for leaves and stems **or** 1 fat eighth of green for leaves and ¾ yard of green Quick Bias for stems
◆ 1 fat eighth each **or** scraps of one gold print and one brown print for sunflowers
◆ 4 yards of brown Quick Bias
◆ ⅞ yard of fabric for backing
◆ 18" x 52" piece of batting
◆ Stabilizer for machine appliqué

Cutting

All measurements include ¼"-wide seam allowance.

From the pale yellow batik, cut:
◆ 1 piece, 15" x 20"
◆ 2 squares, 10½" x 10½"
◆ 2 squares, 8½" x 8½"; cut each square once diagonally to yield 4 corner triangles

From the green print*, cut:
◆ 3 bias strips, each a generous ½" x 12"

From the brown batik, cut:
◆ 3 strips, 2¼" x 42"

*Cut bias strips only if you are making your own bias. Cut the strips just a few threads wider than ½".

Construction

1. Fold the background fabric squares in half twice diagonally to mark the centers, referring to "Transferring the Design" on page 11.

2. Trace the appliqué and/or border designs onto the center of the background squares. To make the project as shown, trace the sunflower wreath pattern on page 88 and the arched-corner border pattern on page 93 sized for a 10" block.

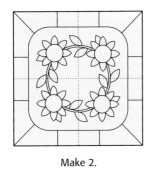

Make 2.

3. Prepare and fuse the border-design fabric onto the background squares or use your favorite method of appliqué, referring to page 13 for details as needed. For machine appliqué, pin or fuse stabilizer to the wrong side of the square to cover the appliqué area. After stitching, remove the stabilizer.

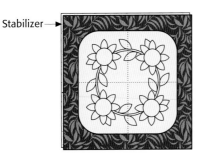

Stabilizer →

4. To make the project as shown, prepare petals for 8 sunflowers (64 total), 8 sunflower centers, and 24 leaves. Apply the bias for the wreath first and stitch in place. Add the leaves and stitch.

5. Add the flowers and stitch around their outer edge. Stitch around the center circle of the sunflowers. Apply and stitch short pieces of bias tape to the arched-corner border; then add bias around the center. Remove stabilizer.

6. Sew the corner triangles to two adjoining sides of the wreath blocks. Apply and stitch bias tape to the long side of each triangle. Add the center rectangle between the wreath block units. Square up the edges of the runner if necessary.

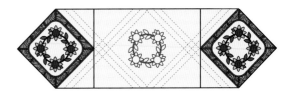

7. To echo the wreath design in the quilting, transfer the appliqué design onto the center panel. Mark any other quilting lines as desired.

8. Prepare the backing by cutting the fabric in half lengthwise and resewing to make a backing approximately 18" x 52". Layer the runner with batting and backing.

9. Quilt as desired. The center wreath was stitched in a variegated thread so the design would stand out.

10. Refer to "French-Twist Binding" on page 23 and follow the directions to add a narrow binding to the table runner.

Hearts and Flowers Table Runner

Finished quilt: 13½" x 61½" ♦ *Finished block: 8" x 8"*
Made by Susan Petruske, 2003, Manchester, Wisconsin.

Susan used synthetic-suede flower wreaths and stained-glass heart wreaths to create this lovely table runner. This design could also double as a long wall quilt for that special narrow space.

Materials

All yardages are based on 42"-wide fabric.

♦ ¾ yard of black print for outer border and binding
♦ ⅝ yard of beige batik for background
♦ ½ yard of tan print for block borders and design centers
♦ 1 fat eighth e*ach* of light blue and dark blue for heart-wreath appliqués
♦ 9" x 12" piece e*ach* of blue and green synthetic suede for wreath appliqués (or cotton fabric)
♦ Scrap of synthetic suede for flower centers (or cotton fabric)
♦ 18 yards of brown Mini Bias for heart wreaths and borders
♦ 2 yards of earth tone Mini Bias for posy wreath
♦ 1 yard of fabric for backing
♦ 17" x 65" piece of batting
♦ Heavyweight fusible web for synthetic suede
♦ Stabilizer for machine appliqué

Cutting

All measurements include ¼"-wide seam allowance.

From the beige batik, cut:
♦ 7 squares, 8½" x 8½"

From the black print, cut:
♦ 4 strips, 3¼" x 42"
♦ 4 strips, 2¼" x 42"

Construction

1. Fold the background fabric squares in half twice to mark the centers, referring to "Transferring the Design" on page 11.

2. Trace the appliqué and border designs sized for an 8" block onto the background squares. Trace the posy wreath pattern on page 87 onto four blocks, the heart wreath pattern on page 90 onto three blocks, and the single-curve border pattern on page 91 onto all blocks. Or use the designs of your choice. Use a stabilizer on the wrong side of each block to cover the appliqué area.

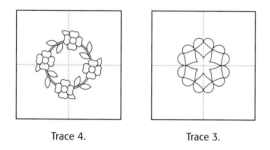

Trace 4.   Trace 3.

3. Prepare and stitch the appliqués. For the posy wreath, prepare four center-design circles, petals for 16 flowers (64 total), 16 flower centers, and 48 leaves. If using synthetic suede, use a no-sew fusible web to eliminate the need to stitch appliqués in place. Position and add the center design of the posy wreath. Apply Mini Bias around the edge of the circle, starting where a flower will cover the raw edges. Stitch the bias tape. Fuse the flowers and leaves into position.

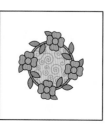

Apply fabric,   Fuse flowers
then bias tape.   and leaves.

4. For the heart wreath, prepare three center star sections, 18 lower-heart sections, and 36 upper-heart sections. Cut the star just slightly oversized to assure coverage when fusing the remaining pieces. Position and apply the center-star design of the heart wreath. Position and fuse the remaining heart pieces. Apply and stitch Mini Bias around the heart motifs, following the arrows in the diagram.

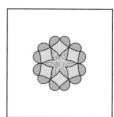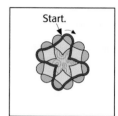

Fuse fabric.   Apply bias tape
in three steps.

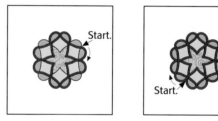

5. Remove the stabilizer from all the blocks when finished stitching.

6. Sew the blocks together, alternating the two different wreaths. Press the seams open.

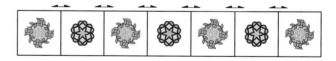

7. Prepare the backing by cutting the fabric in half lengthwise. Sew the pieces together and trim to approximately 17" x 65". Center and layer the blocks onto the batting and backing. Pin baste.

8. Prepare and apply the border fabric for an 8" block. To make a runner like the one in the photograph, cut six double-border sections and 16 single-border sections of the single-curve border. Fuse in place. Then fuse and stitch the Mini Bias to the edges of the interior border.

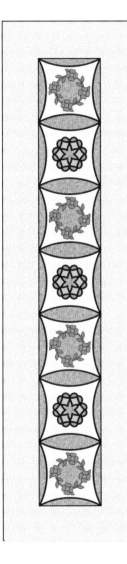

9. Piece the 3¼" outer-border strips together to make one long strip. Refer to "Adding Borders" on page 22 to cut the outer-border strips to the correct length and stitch them to the center of the quilt.

10. Apply and stitch Quick Bias to cover the seam where the outer border was attached, if desired. This will further enhance the stained-glass look.

11. Add additional quilting as desired.

12. Refer to "French-Twist Binding" on page 23 and follow the directions to add narrow binding to the table runner.

TABLE TOPPER
AND TREE SKIRT

This versatile pattern can be made in many sizes. Anything from the smallest tree to a large table can be decorated for the season with this easy-to-piece project. The shape is a nice alternative to traditional rectangular table runners. See the chart on page 81 for cutting dimensions for various sizes.

Silvered Snowflakes Table Topper

Finished quilt: 45" x 45" ♦ *Finished block: 12" x 12"*
Made by Kate Bashynski, 2003, Beaver Dam, Wisconsin.

The snowflake fabric inspired Kate to create this piece to complement her
snowflake ornament collection.

Materials

All yardages are based on 42"-wide fabric.

- 1½ yards of solid blue batik for blocks
- 1 yard of dotted blue batik for block borders and binding
- ⅞ yard of blue snowflake batik for quilt center and borders
- 15 yards of Mini Bias for snowflakes
- 16 yards of Quick Bias for borders
- 1¾ yards of fabric for backing
- 50" x 50" piece of batting

Cutting

All measurements include ¼"-wide seam allowance.

From the solid blue batik, cut:

♦ 6 squares, 12½" x 12½"

♦ 2 strips, 11¼" x 42"; cut into 6 equilateral triangles*

From the blue snowflake batik, cut:

♦ 2 strips, 11¼" x 42"; cut into 6 equilateral triangles*

From the dotted blue batik, cut:

♦ 4 strips, 2¼" x 42"

*See "Cutting Equilateral Triangles" below.

QUICK TIP

To give the table topper a softer feel, use flannel as a backing and eliminate the batting as Kate did.

Cutting Equilateral Triangles

1. Align the 60° line on a 24" ruler with the bottom left edge of a 11¼" solid blue batik strip. Cut off the upper-left corner.

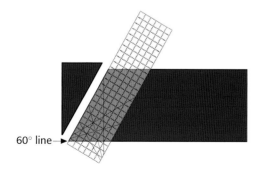

2. Mark the bottom of the strip in increments of 12⅞". Realign the 60° line with the first increment marking so the ruler intersects the top edge at the previous cut. Cut the triangle. Keep track of the straight-grain edges by making a small mark in the seam allowance or inserting a pin along the straight-grain side.

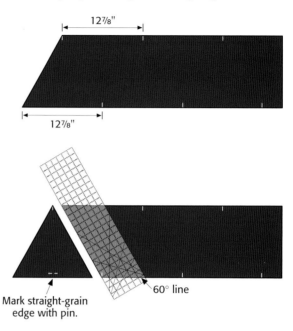

3. Repeat to cut a total of six triangles from the solid blue and six triangles from the snowflake batik.

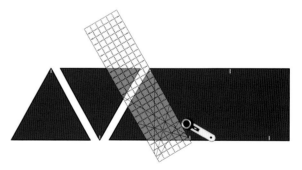

Construction

1. Trace appliqué and/or border designs onto the square and triangle blocks, referring to "Transferring the Design" on page 11. Enlarge snowflake 2 on page 83 by 300% to fit a 12"

square block and enlarge it 125% for the triangle block. The single-curve border on page 91 was also enlarged 300% and traced onto all sides of the square blocks and triangles cut from the solid blue.

Trace 6 each.

QUICK TIP

Depending on the design you choose, you may finish your blocks before sewing them together, or you may sew them together and then add your appliqué and/or border designs.

2. To prepare the border-fabric shapes, cut 12 single-curve border sections from the dotted batik, 6 single-curve border sections from the snowflake batik, and 12 doubled single-curve border sections from the dotted batik. Apply a snowflake border to the top of the square blocks; appliqué a dotted-batik border to the bottom of the square blocks and the triangle blocks as shown, using your preferred method. The adjoining border fabric sections will be added after the blocks are sewn together.

Straight-grain edge
Make 6 each.

3. If you want to add appliqué designs, use a stabilizer on the wrong side of the block behind the area to be stitched. Apply the designs; add bias-tape snowflakes now if you wish. It's easier to add the bias tape around the border areas after layering the table topper. You can then sew the single-curve border in long, continuous curves.

QUICK TIP

Selectively cut a snowflake image from your fabric and appliqué it now if you want to feature it in the center of the large bias snowflake.

4. Sew a square block to the straight-grain side of a snowflake triangle block, matching snowflake fabrics. Repeat with the remaining square blocks. Press seams either open or toward the block on three and toward the triangle on the other three.

5. Sew these sections together as shown. Stop stitching ¼" away from the square blocks where the seams intersect, and backstitch.

Stop stitching ¼" from end and backstitch.

6. To sew the solid blue triangle blocks between the square blocks, you will need to match the point where the seams intersect with the intersection of the previous seams. Once again, be sure that the straight-grain edge of the triangle will be at the outer edge of the skirt. Mark the spot to help with accuracy.

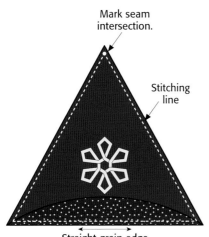

Mark seam intersection.

Stitching line

Straight-grain edge

7. Sew one side of the triangle, beginning at the center and sewing toward the outer edge. Backstitch at the marked point. Do not catch previous seam allowances in stitching.

Start and backstitch.

8. Remove the top from the machine, flip and pivot the triangle to align with the side of the next square; pin and stitch from the center toward the outside. Again, do not catch any seam allowances.

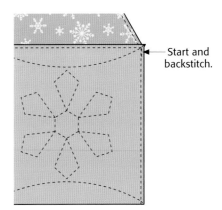

Start and backstitch.

9. Repeat with the remaining sections. Press.

10. Layer with backing and batting or flannel. Pin baste, avoiding the appliqué and border areas.

11. Add the double-border sections between the blocks. Apply Quick Bias tape and appliqués. Stitch in place.

First Bias Application

Second Bias Application

Third Bias Application

QUICK TIP

Use a stitch width wider than the Mini Bias tape to give a lacy look to the outside edges of the tape.

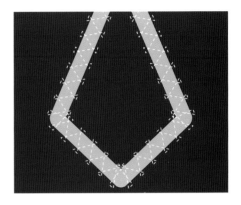

12. Refer to "French-Twist Binding" on page 23 and follow the directions to add narrow binding to the table topper.

Holiday Jewels Tree Skirt

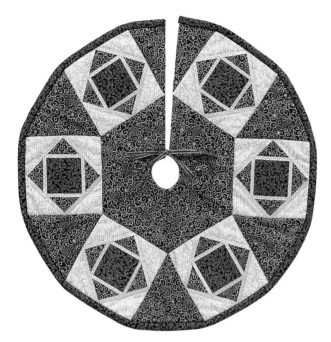

Finished tree skirt: 15" diameter
Finished block: 4" x 4"

All it takes to create this charming small tree skirt is six "Square-in-a-Square" ornaments. Piece them together with sparkling holiday fabrics. Add gold Mini Bias to form jewel-like blocks to surround a miniature Christmas tree.

Materials

All yardages are based on 42"-wide fabric.

- ½ yard of red print for blocks and triangles
- ¼ yard of green print for blocks and binding
- 1 fat quarter of cream print for blocks
- 4 yards of gold Mini Bias
- 1 fat quarter for backing
- 18" x 18" piece of batting

Cutting

All measurements include ¼"-wide seam allowance.

From the cream print, cut:
- 6 squares, 4½" x 4½"

From the red print, cut:
- 6 squares, 3" x 3"
- 2 strips, 4¼" x 21"; cut into 11 equilateral triangles*
- 1 rectangle, 4¾" x 5⅜"

From the green print, cut:
- 6 squares, 2¼" x 2¼"
- 2 strips, 2¼" x 42"

*Refer to "Cutting Equilateral Triangles" on page 74.
The distance along the top and bottom should be 4⅞".*

Construction

1. Make six Square-in-a-Square blocks following steps 1–3 of the instructions for the ornament beginning on page 37. Or use the ornament design of your choice to make six blocks. Do not layer with batting until the tree skirt top is assembled. Add the bias tape before assembly

so the raw edges of the bias will be caught in the seams. If you are using another design for the blocks, determine whether the bias and appliqués should be added now or in step 11.

2. Cut the triangle sections for the tree skirt opening from the 4¾" x 5⅜" rectangle. Align the 60° line on your ruler with the bottom left edge of the rectangle; cut as shown. Realign the 60° line in the opposite direction on the other side of the rectangle so the ruler intersects the top edge of the previous cut.

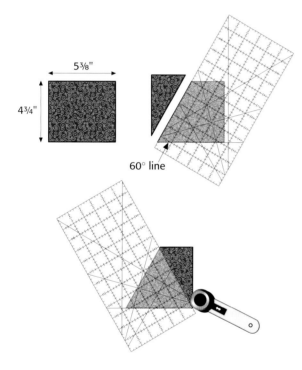

60° line

3. Cut down the center of the triangle lengthwise to form two half triangles.

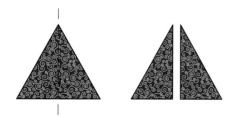

4. Follow steps 4–9 for the table topper, beginning on page 75, sewing the sections together as shown. Leave one seam open.

Leave open.

5. Add the half triangles from step 3 to the remaining edges. Press thoroughly. Trim the bottom of the triangles even with the blocks, if necessary.

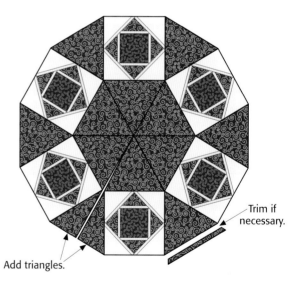

Add triangles.

Trim if necessary.

6. Cut the fat quarter for the backing down the middle and stitch from one end to the center, right sides together. Press the seam open. For other sizes, the backing should be 2" wider than the finished width of the skirt.

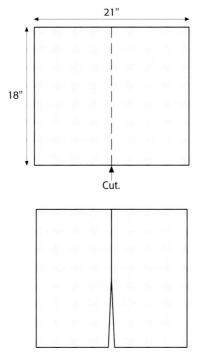

21"

18"

Cut.

Stop stitching at center.

7. Layer the batting, backing, and tree skirt top, with the batting on the bottom. The backing and tree skirt should be right sides together with the opening edges even. Pin the opening edges together.

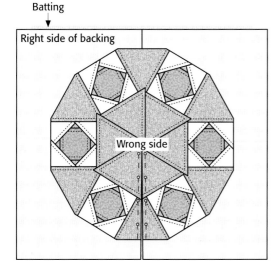

Batting

Right side of backing

Wrong side

8. Decide how large you want the opening to be. Natural trees need a much larger opening than artificial trees. Draw a circle in the appropriate size on top of the wrong side of the tree skirt top.

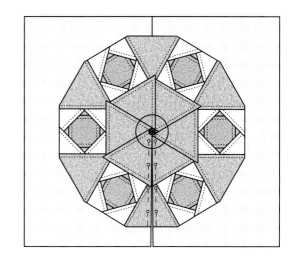

QUICK TIP

Center a round template on top of the center of the tree skirt and mark around it with a water-soluble marker. When the template is removed, adjust the circle as necessary.

---

9. Begin stitching at the outer edge along the opening using a ¼"-wide seam allowance; stitch around the center circle on the drawn line and down the other opening. Trim away the center circle ¼" to the inside of the

stitched line. Clip closely along the curve up to the stitching line but do not cut into the stitching.

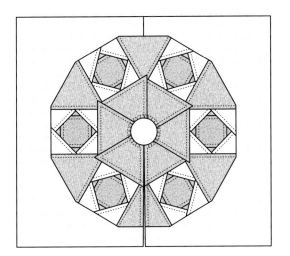

10. Turn the tree skirt top right side out through the opening and press. The batting should now be layered between the tree skirt top and the backing. Pin baste..

11. Apply bias tape and any appliqués if not already done in step 1. Stitch in place.

12. Quilt as desired. Trim the excess batting and backing even with the edge of the tree skirt.

13. Refer to "French-Twist Binding" on page 23and follow the directions to add a narrow binding to the outer edges of the tree skirt. Trim the binding about ¼" from the tree skirt

CUTTING FOR TABLE TOPPERS AND TREE SKIRTS IN VARYING SIZES

Table Topper or Tree Skirt Finished Diameter	Finished Block Size	Size to Cut Six Squares for Blocks	Strip Width to Cut for Equilateral Triangles	Increment Length for Equilateral Triangles*	Size to Cut Tree-Skirt Opening Rectangle
15"	4"	4½"	4¼"	4⅞"	4¾" x 5⅜"
22½"	6"	6½"	6"	6⅞"	6½" x 7⅜"
30"	8"	8½"	7¾"	8⅞"	8¼" x 9⅜"
37½"	10"	10½"	9½"	10⅞"	10" x 11⅜"
45"	12"	12½"	11¼"	12⅞"	11¾" x 13⅜"

*Cut 12 equilateral triangles for the table topper; cut 11 for the tree skirt.
See "Cutting Equilateral Triangles" on page 74.

openings. Fold to the inside before hand stitching the binding to the back, as shown.

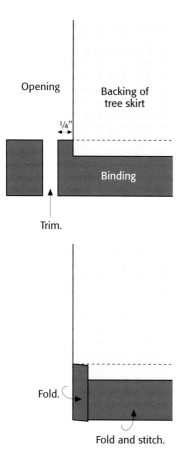

14. If desired, add ribbon or fabric ties to the center opening edge to tie the tree skirt around the tree.

DESIGN OPTION

Make a sweet Easter table topper to welcome spring into your home. Place a bouquet of spring flowers or basket of colored eggs in the center to complete your holiday decor.

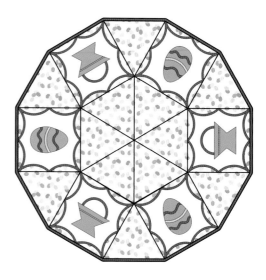

Appliqué and Bias Design Patterns

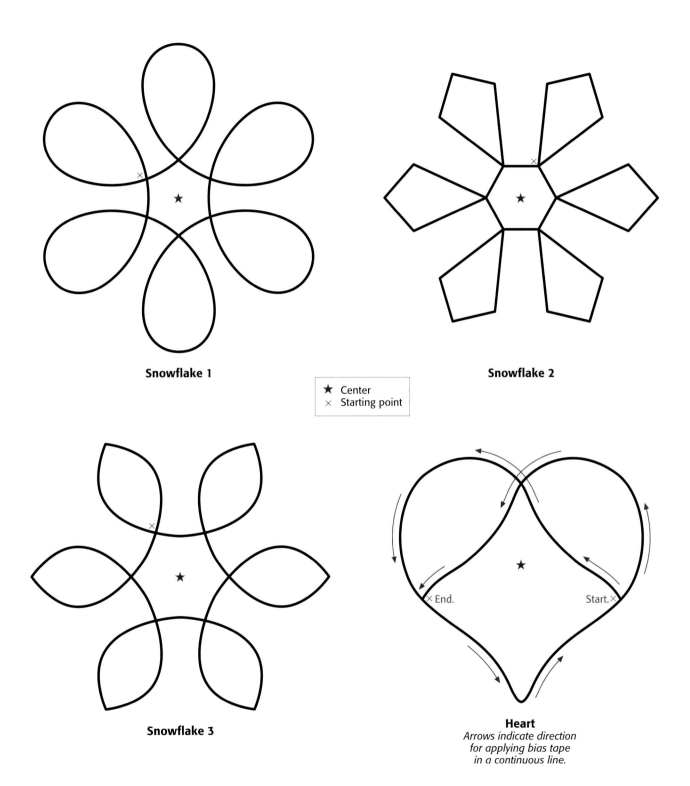

Snowflake 1

★	Center
×	Starting point

Snowflake 2

Snowflake 3

Heart
*Arrows indicate direction
for applying bias tape
in a continuous line.*

× End.   Start. ×

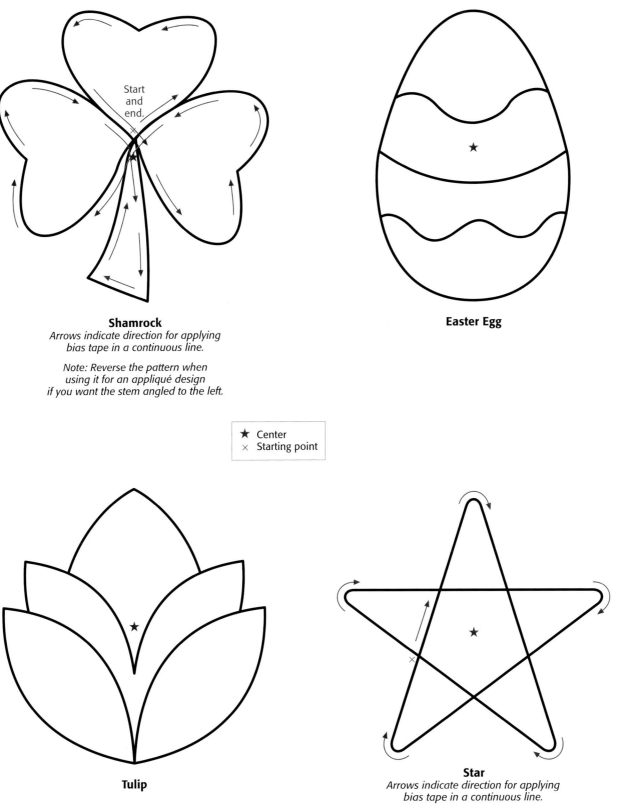

Shamrock
*Arrows indicate direction for applying
bias tape in a continuous line.*

*Note: Reverse the pattern when
using it for an appliqué design
if you want the stem angled to the left.*

Easter Egg

★ Center
× Starting point

Tulip

Star
*Arrows indicate direction for applying
bias tape in a continuous line.*

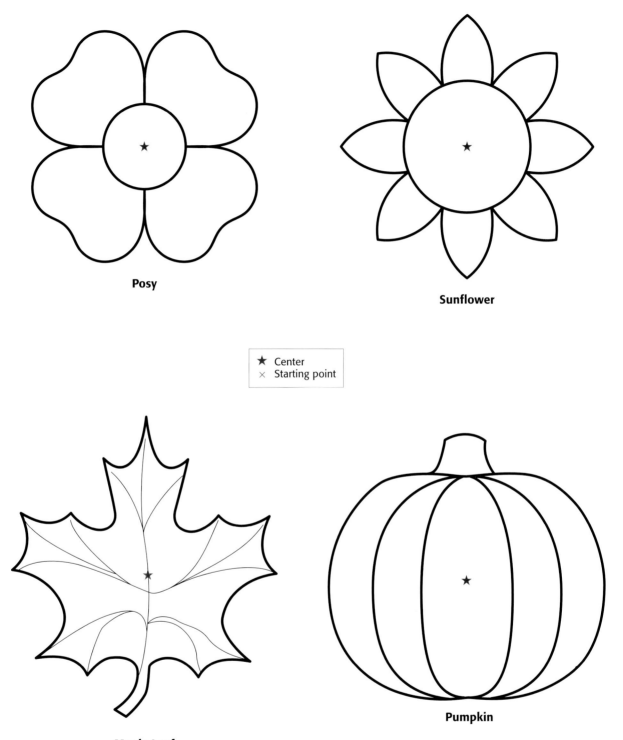

Posy

Sunflower

★ Center
× Starting point

Maple Leaf
Vein lines are optional.

Pumpkin

Basket

Celtic Rose
*Arrows indicate direction
for applying bias tape
in a continuous line.*

★ Center
× Starting point

Start
and end.

Start and end.

Medallion

Cut 16.

Cut 4.

Cut 12.

★ Center

Posy Wreath

★ Center

Cut 32.

Cut 4.

Cut 12.

Sunflower Wreath

Tulip Wreath

★Center

Heart Wreath

Border Patterns

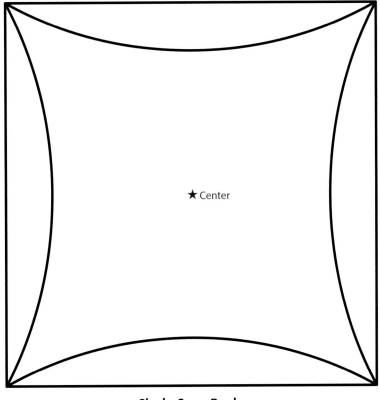

★ Center

Single-Curve Border
4" Block

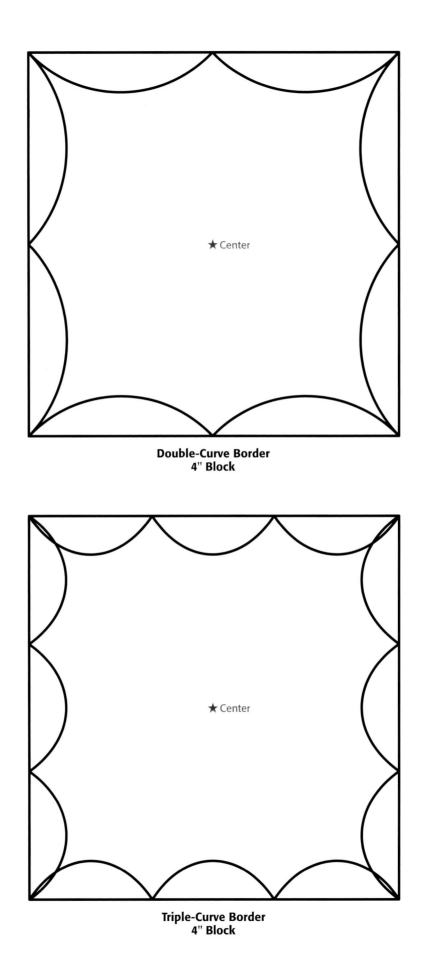

★Center

Double-Curve Border
4" Block

★Center

Triple-Curve Border
4" Block

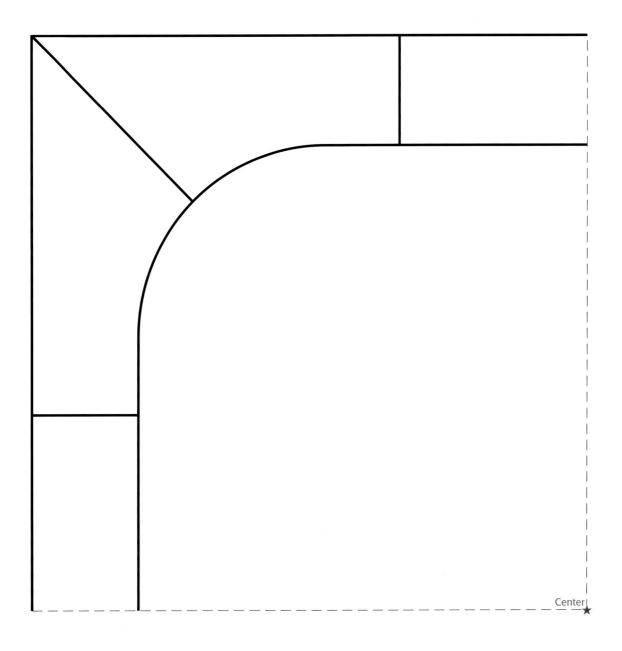

Arched-Corner Border
12" Block
Make 4.

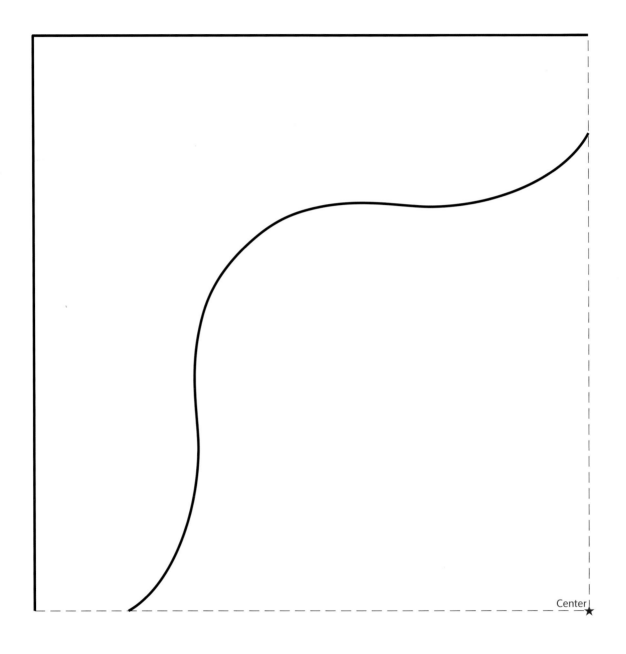

Center ★

Graceful-Curves Border
12" Block
Make 4.

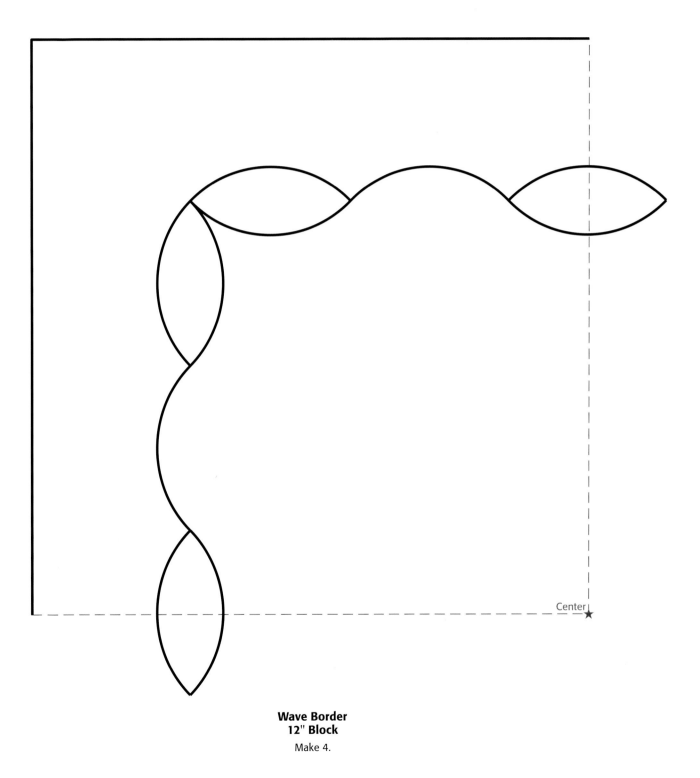

Wave Border
12" Block

Make 4.

Resources

Connecting Threads
P.O. Box 8940
Vancouver, WA 98668-8940
800-574-6454
www.connectingthreads.com

Nancy's Notions
P.O. Box 683
333 Beichl Avenue
Beaver Dam, WI 53916-0683
800-833-0690
www.nancysnotions.com

Nancy's Notions carries general quilting and sewing supplies as well as the specialized supplies needed for making the projects in this book.

About the Author

Gretchen Hudock began sewing at the age of 10 under the direction of her mother. With three older sisters also sewing, her time at the machine was limited. An introductory course in textiles while at the University of Wisconsin intrigued her enough to want to major in the field. "I did not know what I was going to do with the degree, but I was going to enjoy myself." Gretchen had never taken an art course before attending college, and she discovered that while art was time consuming, it did not seem like work. To this day, Gretchen loves creating and "playing" with fabric. The computer now helps streamline the design process.

Gretchen was introduced to quilting while watching public television. She began designing Christmas tree skirts, and one thing led to another;

Christmas quilts became her specialty. She has had many designs published nationally and has been a guest on public television's *Sewing with Nancy*. Since 1995, Gretchen has been the quilting consultant for Nancy's Notions, where she designs catalog projects, tests new products, and promotes quilting wherever possible. This is her second book on the subject of Quick Bias.

Gretchen lives in Slinger, Wisconsin, with her husband, Rich. Their two children, John and Elizabeth, will be out of college when this book is printed, but the new family dog, Farley, helps keep life interesting. "I have truly been blessed to be able to do what I love to do as a job. It is wonderful to look forward to each workday."